**REVISED FOR THE NEW MILLENNIUM**

# Work for a Living

and

# Still Be Free To Live!

## Eileen McDargh

© 2007 Loch Lomond Press

First Printing 2007
Second Printing 2008
Third Printing 2010

ISBN 978-0-9623190-6-8

Original cover illustration by John "vStyler" Gordon. You can see more of his work at his website MaxStyles.com, URL: http://www.maxstyles.com/

Many thanks to LightStar Technologies for their assistance and gracious help with this art.

Book Design by Whitney Campbell & Co.
207-846-0768

Eileen McDargh

Eileen is a certified speaking professional (CSP) and her election into the CPAE Speaker Hall of Fame places her among the top 3% of the 3500-member National Speakers Association. She's on the Board of Directors of NSA and also on the national board for Take Back Your Time, an international initiative for work/life integration practices.

To Contact Eileen:
E-mail: eileen@eileenmcdargh.com
Web: EileenMcDargh.com

# TABLE OF CONTENTS

# Introduction

*"The more things change, the more some things remain the same..."*
*– Anon*

Since the last revision of this book in 1999, the world has changed dramatically. From terrorism to tsunamis, from global warming to war zones, from exponential off shoring to expeditious downsizing, we're slapped with the fragility of life and the fiction of security. Even this book was an inconsequential victim of terrorism. My publisher went into Chapter 11 bankruptcy following 9/11 and the remaining books eventually found their way to my garage.

For an author, it's a hard decision: pull the plug or attempt resuscitation. That's the "normal" course for writers. But more and more of my clients not only asked for the book, they wanted keynotes and retreats built upon its themes. In the face of breathless change, I realized that what remained the same but intensified, was a desire for meaningful work and a sustainable life against the backdrop of insecurity.

So, I decided on a third approach: deconstruct and remodel. I've pulled out major sections because the entire notion of "balance" deserves more than a few chapters. Deconstruction was essential. (Watch for my new book which will explode the myths of balance and present an expanded model for handling the demands of an unequal life.)

The remodel is designed to streamline your ability to grasp ideas quickly and to take charge of wherever you find yourself today in the world of work. If there's one theme that runs throughout it's the notion of SELF-LEADERSHIP, of leading yourself to a place where YOU transform the life of business and the business of your life. It's about using case studies to demonstrate how YOU can take action to either amend, alter, abandon, or accept where you find yourself in the world of work. "Accept", by the way, is not resignation but a mindful decision that makes the most sense for current reality.

For this reason, you will find many choices in the book. Only choices. The answers must come from you. Some readers will find an affirmation, a giant "yes" to present or future plans. Others might gather ideas for deconstructing and remodeling work processes. Still others might be heartened to see themselves in a segment of the working population that transcends traditional labels, job descriptions, and pigeon holes.

Some books are read with the mind and others with the heart.
This will require both.

# Chapter One:
# **Back to the Drawing Board**

*Never for the sake of peace and quiet deny*
*your own feelings or experiences.*

*— Dag Hammarskjold*

Brilliantly said. Harder to do.

For many of us, the spinning circle of work, external pressures and internal agendas cram our twenty-four hours so full that we rarely take time to question why there's a sense of emptiness or loss of control in our lives. Or why we find ourselves getting up for work and saying, "Good God, morning!" instead of, "Good morning, God."

Consider this book your time out. And more.

If your day is partitioned into gray segments of work/eat/sleep—if you have to introduce yourself before having dinner with your children—if the business is running you instead of you running the business—if your soul hungers for a deeper meaning to life—you NEED more.

If your family and friends think you've flown over the cuckoo's nest when you wistfully talk about leaving your executive position for a country store in Snohomish, WA—if your last significant relationship was with your seventh-grade flame and you're too busy "working" to even remember his/her name—then there's a big hole in your todays that will dramatically impact your tomorrows.

Some of you have become entrepreneurs struggling to launch new businesses. For the survivors in shrinking firms, the workload hasn't diminished just because the work force got smaller. A second shift of at-home labor begins after regular work hours. Meals have turned toward grazing. We now microwave everything and have lost the magic of the kitchen. Technology tracks us from boardrooms to bedrooms to bathrooms. We work everywhere.

If you can identify with any of these scenarios, it's time to head back to the drawing board. And you won't be alone. People are redesigning their jobs all over the place.

Look at some of the marvelous books which have jumped off the shelves in the last seven years: *The Purpose-Driven Life* (Rick Warren); *What Should I Do with My Life* (Po Bronson); *Love It. Don't Leave It.* (Bev Kaye and Sharon Jordan-Evans); *Making a Life. Making a Living* (Mark Albion); *Passion at Work* (Lawler Kang) and a host of others.

These books mirror the essence of our common dilemma. How do we swim with the sharks, grow a business, earn a living and still claim lives of wholeness and quality? The evidence is mounting: for far too many of us, work seems to be working us. The packed agendas of our days result in life leading us rather than us leading a life. Now more than ever we seek to know how to work for a living and still be free to live.

Consider this your encouragement. You are not alone.

There are, quite frankly, a lot of us in just such a spot, slugging it out in a vacuum and looking for something or someone to tell us, "you're not crazy." It becomes apparent that just the simple sharing of experiences brings tremendous relief and support.

And so this is a lima bean book. It has grown from the seed of my work experiences and research into a supportive guide for individuals seeking balance within their careers and more to life than a paycheck. It has been fertilized by the candid life/work histories of teachers, corporate executives, entrepreneurs, medical professionals, engineers, athletes, artists, and others. And it has been warmed by an eagerness to relay a pattern for coming to terms with twenty-first-century business reality and personal needs.

Throughout the years as I have struggled to find my niche in the world of work, I've discovered numerous other professionals in a wide variety of fields and economic strata agonizing over the same questions: "Is this all there is to life?" "What do I really want to do?" From listening to their steps in handling such a dilemma and from comparing it to my experience, five things are now clear:

1. There are distinct stages to the process of answering these questions.

2. A new definition of "work" has emerged.

3. Honest personal evaluation is essential and probably the hardest task.

4. The essence of successful living is integration: a delicate weaving of intellectual, material, physical, emotional, and spiritual ingredients into our lives.

5. The work/life solutions of today will have to change as we grow and change. But if we understand the process (and how some other people handled it), hopefully the next phase won't be so overwhelming.

If only I had known these things way back when ... when life had as much gusto as stale beer ... when the corporate vice president accepted my resignation and said, "You're making a big mistake" ... when self-doubt and depression slapped my wrist. If only I had known there were others going through the same process ... that it is a process, a transactional unfolding of me which will be repeated again and again. If only....

I am writing this book to correct those "if-onlys."

Because all of us must respond to the demands of life in our own unique way, I'd like to think that this book contains a smorgasbord of ideas. Please take what appeals to you; leave the rest behind. I only ask that you allow yourself to mentally sample each section. Open yourself to the possibility that there just might be another mind-set for approaching your work.

# Chapter Two
# This Thing Called "Work"

*"To find out what one is fitted to do, and to secure an opportunity to do it, is the key to happiness."*

*– John Dewey*

When American philosopher and educational reformer John Dewey died in 1952, this statement was viewed as admirable but unattainable. Work was more commonly equated with income production and output. Lots of output. The prevailing thought in the post WWII world was, "You got a job. Shut up and be happy".

Doesn't work that way any more.

Fast forward and you will find an exploding field of career coaches, all committed to helping you find "fit". Organizations struggle to engage and retain talent, often failing in the process. Survey after survey points to a significant dissatisfaction with the pace, place, and personality of the work environment. A comprehensive poll, sponsored by 24 leading U.S. companies, and by Harris Interactive, Inc. for Age Wave, an independent think tank, concluded that:

Across the American workforce, only 45 percent of workers say they are satisfied, (33 percent), or extremely satisfied, (12 percent), with their jobs. At the same time, a much lower number actually feel very "engaged" by their jobs; Only 20 percent feel very passionate about their jobs; less than 15 percent agree that they feel strongly energized by their work; and only 31 percent (strongly or moderately) believe that their employer inspires the best in them.

Magazine article after magazine article bemoans the lack of energy, loyalty, and enthusiasm. We're told that morale equals motivation. So, while managers look for ways to motivate employees, employees wait for the organizations to turn them on. Neither is doable.

Motivation is an inside-out job. It's like dandruff: it's in your head. Self-motivation is redundant. There is no other kind. Stop waiting to take charge of your happiness. You have more control than you think.

Imagine the sense of personal power if you could discover ways to control your response to your current job environment while freeing yourself to make more authentic career decisions. Imagine the release you would feel if you could turn work fixation into fascination, and make a reconnection with the rest of life.

Let's explore some current shifts in the workplace which will influence that flip from fixation into fascination.

## Shift #1: A Move Away From Employment Guarantees

The old social contract between companies and workers is dead and buried. Traditional notions of lifelong employment, guaranteed retirement, and clearly defined job ladders have faded into the sunset.

Cover after cover of business magazines speak about the demise of "the job."

Shifts like this often strike terror into hearts. After all, while this might not have been the job of our dreams, it was at least a paycheck. As with any life event, we have two choices: complain about the shift or create a personal game plan to deal with reality. Career resiliency and lack of job permanence can be an opportunity. No longer must you wait for some blessing from on high to develop skills, market yourself, and take more responsibility for your own welfare.

## Shift #2: You have a life outside of work

Programs designed to help employees juggle the demands of their work and personal lives continue to grow in popularity. In a number of corporations, work/family programs offer everything from childcare assistance, to on-site exercise classes, and concierge services. Acknowledging the aging boomer population, elder care is slowly being added to benefit programs along with flexible scheduling. Corporate sabbaticals are spreading. No longer the privilege of academics and senior executives, they're becoming a valuable tool in recruitment and retention.

One of the criteria for selection as one of the 100 Best Workplaces in America, is work/life integration programs. At the same time, knowing work/life integration is important and operating on it are two different things.

Case in point: During a conversation, the president of a large consulting firm admitted privately that a job applicant was turned down because he was too involved with Little League and family affairs to put in the unspoken requisite of sixty hours per week. "And you know, Eileen," concluded the president, "I expect my employees to place company responsibilities first."

Now don't think that I'm discounting the reality that employees frequently put in long hours. Goodness knows I can't even begin to count the days when I was the first one in a corporate office and one of the last to leave. But to make a conscious decision that work must always take precedence over other things in life is to deny a fully human existence.

Not only do we hunger for human contact within our jobs, but if living is our goal, we require time for the significant people in our lives and for ourselves. Getting a gold watch for putting in thirty years and sixty hours a week at the same company no longer holds appeal. We want more from both inside and outside our place of employment. In fact, a nationally recognized testing instrument used to assess the internal health of an organization now uses the amount of employee free time as one of the measures for a productive environment.

## Shift #3: A Move Toward Variety and Importance

Is your life the same now as it was ten years ago? Are you the same person you were ten years ago? How about five? Three? Maybe even yesterday? If you answered yes to the above, you either have been a victim of cryogenics or have been recently returned by some closely encountered group from Asteroid B-27.

Our lives are radically changed by the nanosecond speed world we now inhabit. The computer I have today is obsolete by tomorrow. Web knowledge puts data at our fingertips within seconds. Our voice and image transmits over wireless networks. New jobs and titles spring forth every day, boggling the mind with their implications: chief of disruption, innovation finance department, and more.

The implication for the world of work is that we are easily bored, stifled, and discontent with rigid environments. There is too much change around us for the static, the regimented, and—for many of us—the unimportant. We want to count, to have it matter that somewhere in a picture that's larger than ourselves, our life is significant.

These shifts, I think, account for the fact that we often feel like we're in a tailspin, wanting more in our lives than just punching a clock.

It has been said that we fear not death, but death with insignificance. The biggest shift in the American work force is a yearning for meaning in what we do. As that classic work writer, Studs Terkel, concluded decades ago, "Most of us have jobs that are too small for our spirits."

---

*We work to become, not to acquire*
*– Elbert Hubbard*

---

## Let's Throw Webster Out the Window

With these shifts, I think we need to redefine just what work is and is not.

Let's start with the obvious. An old Irish proverb defines work as, "the yeast that raises dough." Granted, some of us might end up with massive loaves and others with pita bread, but earning money is certainly a real portion to our definition.

At first glance, the tendency is to place primary emphasis on this definition: "Work is what one gets paid for." Why else would more women now be employed outside the home than at any previous time in our history?

Right???

Wrong. According to a New York Times poll, the majority of American women believe that their place is on the job; that work and independence are elements of life as satisfying as spouses, homes, and children. In fact, even if they could afford it, 58 percent of U.S. working women said they would rather work than stay at home.

There must be something more to work than pay.

Jean Paul Sartre, the Nobel award-winning author, struck mental gold when he claimed that work was "the significance of an individual."

Check it out at any cocktail party. The conversation will probably go like this: "Hi, my name is John. I'm a neighbor of Pete and Jan's. I saw you standing by the chopped liver and thought I'd come over and get acquainted."

"Er, my name is Eileen." (If it's me, I'm mumbling through a mouthful of pate and cracker.)

"Well, what do you do?"

There you have it. My significance, my identity is now coming from the work that I do. What dear John is REALLY asking is, "Who are you?" It's not that he's being sly or circumspect. After all, if he did ask me who I was, chances are I'd reply with, "I'm a management consultant and a speaker." Even I define myself in such terms.

Still doubt the power of work to give us identity?

Imagine you are unemployed and cocktail-party John asks that question. Would a hot flush zoom up your neck as you reply, "I'm currently exploring alternatives?" Would you cross your fingers and state, "I'm independently wealthy?"

One in-between-jobs executive told me that she felt worthless and small when confronted with such questions.

A business editor who had just been notified of his publication's demise, responded even more strongly", I'm now a nobody. As an editor I had clout. Could get in anywhere; talk with anyone. Who's going to give the time of day to just untitled me?"

For these people, and for many of us, work even has power over our self-esteem and our personal sense of who we are!

In his landmark book, Work and Love: The Crucial Balance, Dr. Jay B. Rohrlich confirms this fact:

"There are many kinds of self symbols: feelings, interests, loves, memories, opinions, tastes, clothing styles, national heritages, religions, material possessions, memberships, etc. But to give uniqueness to an individual, one relies most fully on one's 'piece of work.' All other associations are more passive expressions of self than what we do."

Unfortunately, too often we select work because the title has character and immediate recognition. But is that job, that title, what really brings out our true sense of self? Now more than ever, Sartre's explanation is a valid part in our new "work" definition.

I think a blend of both is the answer. The definition I prefer came from a sprightly woman with over seventy years of living and learning to her credit: "A job is what you do for money. Work is what you do for a life."

Ahh. What insight!

She continued, "'Work' is what energizes, gives meaning and significance to the very unique talents we all possess. Life then becomes the balance of all those essential physical, emotional, material, mental, and spiritual components that create a life worth truly living."

I got the message.

## Here's Our New Definition

To rephrase my dear septuagenarian: Work is that significant, energizing activity which provides meaning to life. It is not necessarily the source of livelihood, but it is, most assuredly, that which makes you alive.

You have a special talent, a unique gift, a definite role to play on Planet Earth which is yours and yours alone. Whether you've reached the place on Life's stage in which it is time to move into an entirely different role for Act II or Act III, or you're standing in the wings auditioning for a part, you are gifted.

In simple terms, your gift—what I consider to be your real work—is that energizing activity during which time melts away as you become absorbed in the "doing." You burn on all four burners and despite probable challenges, there is a sense of accomplishment, passion, and purpose. It might be as straightforward as shelving books at the library or as complex as writing software programs to monitor trajectory patterns for space vehicles. As career coach and author, Barbara Sher insists, "It means getting what you want. Not what your father or mother wanted for you, not what you think you can realistically get in this world, but what you want."

Think of the implications within this definition: Many of us might have "jobs" but no work! Imagine what energizes, challenges, and excites you. Why, it might be any number of things from the most complex down to the simplest: designing software, singing, gardening, counseling, working with tools, telling children's stories, exploring new cities, selling a product, balancing ledger sheets, baking cookies, saving souls.

Is your energizing "work" part of your job? Do you even know what that "work" is? Is your life so out of kilter that you wouldn't know "work" from "job" if it whistled Yankee Doodle?

Whatever it is, the role of this book is to give you support and permission (which ultimately you must give to yourself) to make choices which will create a sustainable life, allowing you to live and "work" at the same time.

But it's not easy. The not-free-to-live feeling comes as a result of one or more of the following:

1. We are spending so much time at our "job" that there is nothing left for our "work" as well as our personal life.

2. We are spending so much energy at our "work" that we're disconnected from other vital life components.

3. We don't know what our "work" is.

4. We don't know (or won't accept) that we can integrate and weave varied parts of our life.

5. We are afraid to risk and change.

6. We are afraid of the future.

7. We set limits on ourselves.

8. We see ourselves as powerless.

In the long run, the ultimate task is to make "job" and "work" synonymous. Even that's not an easy chore. For one thing, most of us don't consider such mingling to be possible.

During my first year as a consultant, I found myself accepting public-relations clients seeking publicity. Although I had well-established credentials and could easily handle the assignments, something was wrong.

Ah hah! I soon realized that the reason I started out on my own was not to start a public-relations agency, but to handle communication problems which I found more meaningful: training in interpersonal skills; analyzing and developing a smooth communication flow between management and employees; speaking. I felt no energy in getting someone's face on prime-time television.

Suddenly, I knew why I kept turning down some clients, accepting others; doubting one day and believing the next; receiving conflicting feelings from my stomach and my heart. Instinctively, I was aiming at my "work" and not a "job". But the bank balance and old mental tapes were pushing me into accepting "jobs" instead of concentrating on my "work."

I'm still struggling. But along the way have come some insights about this process of "working" and "living." For example, I now know we might have to accept a "job" until such times as we can do our "work." Or, we might keep a "job" in order to support our "work." I can readily see that our choice of everything from material possessions to physical exercise impacts the balance and calm surrounding either "work" or a "job."

But I also have learned that we have absolute freedom (and therefore responsibility) to choose what goes into our life and to choose how we feel about that life.

The problem is that frequently we don't know what powerful choices we have. In fact, we might not even wish to examine our lives because we see ourselves as formed in concrete and without opportunity for change.

It seems hidden attitudes get in the way.

## Some Stumbling Blocks to Working and Living

No matter how old we are, we carry attitudes with us: attitudes about ourselves, work, other people, and the world in general. Not all attitudes are healthy. Some might keep us from really growing, changing, and deeply living. Since our current employment is where we concentrate at least one-half of our waking time, it stands to reason that these attitudes will probably be expressed within our job. Some of these attitudes, attached to us with mental super glue, can prevent us from honestly looking at our present work. Just as soon as we start to question where we are—zap—the attitude becomes a force field that throws us back into inaction.

Sit back now and reflect if you might possibly be holding any of these attitudes. If you are, for the time being, merely acknowledge that fact.

## Attitude One: I Cannot Waste What I Was Educated to Do

Amazing what a piece of sheepskin can do to promote immobility. Not surprising, though. Most of us worked extremely hard, at great financial risk, to gain the educational objective we fixed our star upon when we were in our late teens and early twenties.

Why did we choose what we did? Robert W., a psychotherapist, received this very clear message from his Russian-immigrant parents, "I think I was five when I heard my mother introduce me to her friends as, "This is Robert. He'll be a doctor." My uncle was a physician and, to my parents, wherever God was, Uncle Zeke was four steps above Him. I grew up on stories of Uncle Z, struggling through the snow in winter to become a doctor; paying back my grandparents by cleaning spittoons. It was very much a matter of success and paying back my parents for whatever they sacrificed. When I told Mama I didn't want to be a doctor, she looked at Grandmama, shrugged her shoulders and said, "Well, you must follow your heart—so you'll be a dentist."

It's funny now when Robert tells the story. But little humor came with the original message—without those careers, Robert would never make it.

"Making it" seemed to play a heavy role in the majority of academic decisions. Which professions earned substantial incomes? Which professions would be in demand at graduation? Which professions would bring a beaming nod of approval from our societal and/or familial group, influenced—and still do—the choice of higher degrees?

And probably, for many of us, we did hit upon something that we liked to do ... at that time in our lives.

Having taught school and been guilty of asking students what they will be when they grow up, I can only beg for mercy and plead temporary insanity for asking that question. After personal trial and error, let the truth be known: I'm going to be lots of things when I grow up! (And I'm not finished growing.)

Doesn't that make better sense? You are not the same person today as you were fifteen years ago. Perhaps you've uncovered new talents, other interests, and your college education seems only mildly relative to what you'd really like to do.

The higher the education, the harder it will be to overturn this attitude. Ronda S., a speech therapist, whose story you will encounter later, acknowledged that for some time she kept ignoring thoughts of discontent and change because "I was already trained. What else did I know how to do? Why, I figured it would be crazy to throw away what I had learned."

Even if you succeed in convincing yourself to explore alternatives, society seems to have a hard time with it. "After I took a leave of absence from the school and began to explore other possibilities, more often than not, prospective employers would look at me in disbelief and ask why I was doing something as foolish as considering leaving my profession," recalled Ronda.

The NASA engineer-turned-artist, the chemist-turned-management-consultant, the ophthalmologist-turned-novelist are but a scattering of the people I've interviewed who had to acknowledge and change such an attitude in order to put true work in their lives.

## Attitude Two: To Be a Success, I Must Make a Lot of Money

Once upon a time it was enough to have a chicken in every pot. Now, you better add every bit of technology, home entertainment, jazzy car, and those $400 designer jeans with holes in the knees. Yes, it all takes money. The problem is, the money begins to control us rather than the other way around.

In one sense, our attitude toward money might be part of our nation's inheritance. The Calvinist work ethic not only urged our founding fathers to put their noses to the grindstone, but also proclaimed financial bounty as a "blessing" from the Most High.

Some of this attitude might also have come from personal or parental experience with the Great Depression. Never before in the history of our nation had survival been such an issue. What money could buy was critical.

Is there any wonder that the deep recessions of the last twenty years may have triggered a nightmare memory for many people? Or if we don't remember the Depression, there are those who call it to mind.

During a recent economic downturn, whenever I made a long distance call to my Mother, she inevitably ended the conversation with this warning: "Don't call me. Save your money. You'll never know when this will get worse." It's hard not to have that ghost-of-bad-times-past rub off and to become fearful about one's future solvency.

Unfortunately, rather than needing money for survival, I have found it more common that money is needed for "things"—or at least to give the impression of "things." I'd be willing to bet a diamond ring that we all know a business-woman (or man) who drives a top-of-the-line Lamborghini, wears designer clothes, insists on first-class airline seats, and lives in the exclusive residential community. However, get them in conversation and you'll find they live in fear: afraid that something will happen to the growing business. Why, they might lose the car! Or the estate! But ... in the process of the job (or maybe even "work"), they have also lost contact with children, the spouse is but a distant memory, and there are no close friends. Feeding the lifestyle dragon created tremendous imbalance. Simple question: Is this success? Is this living? Was it worth it?

According to New York clinical psychologist, Dr. Jeffrey Blum, money just doesn't buy happiness. Based upon his personal experience and also his work as a therapist in community clinics and posh psychiatric facilities for the very affluent, he reached this conclusion about money: "More than anything else, money resembles cocaine. You can never have enough; you need more to get the same high; it leaves you depressed and it is overrated."

The problem comes when making money, rather than making a life, becomes the single reason for hopping out of bed in the morning.

## Attitude Three: Money is the Root of All Evil and I'll Be a Bad Person If I Make Too Much

Here's the flip side of Attitude Two. It's one that can be just as damaging and keep us from honestly looking at our work and the thing we call "living."

Those of us who didn't get the Calvinist message heard another one. Namely, it is easier for a camel to waddle through the needle's eye than for a rich person to find heavenly happiness. Then too, let's not forget the all-too-human trait of disparaging those who have what we would really like. If we came from a family that perceived itself to be on the lower economic rung, the eternal antagonism between the haves and the have-nots might be a constant refrain that haunts our subconscious.

To make matters worse, quite a few of us decided that we weren't doing enough to deserve more money; that we'd look greedy and selfish if we asked for more; that if we were in a service position like social work or teaching, the benefits should be heartfelt and not pocket-felt.

Personally, it has taken me quite some time to acknowledge that it is okay to be substantially paid for what I do; that money, kept in its proper perspective, is okay and—as the commercial says—I'm worth it! Now, the criteria for how much work and how much money is directly related to the way in which I define the value and quality of my service. But until I realized that I was influenced by such an attitude, I was not honestly looking at my work/life.

Attitudes Two and Three seem to cause the most hang-ups in examining not only our current work/job, but also in determining our future actions. But we'll talk more about money later.

## Attitude Four: If I Make a Mistake, I'm No Good

Looking at where you are in life and where you are going is risky business. After all, the mirror on the wall might call for change. There's something warm and easy about staying exactly where you are in life. Don't rattle the cage. Put more layers of mental insulation around your feelings. Stay safe because what if you make a move and—horrors—you make a mistake. You were wrong. You were better off where you were.

Granted, choices which dramatically impact others must be made with moral and ethical considerations. One doesn't just close down a manufacturing plant, fire employees, and run to Bora Bora because life needs a change. Nor does one place the family fortune on Gallant Steed to place in the third, lose, and walk away saying, "Oh well, such is life." These choices can be big, big mistakes.

However, when the above attitude is one that prevents personal growth, it's a sure-fire guarantee that juices will dry up and you'll turn into a dull, shriveled individual. If you take nothing more from this book, at least allow yourself to recognize the harm in holding such an attitude about yourself close to your fearful heart.

In fact, I like the mind-set of a gutsy woman writer in her late forties who came to Hollywood with about $1,500 in her pocket, a teenaged daughter, and only the vague inclination of a potential job. When challenged by well-meaning friends about this very obvious wrong move, she'd retort: "There's no such thing as mistakes, only choices from which we learn, grow, and advance."

She was convinced, despite the gloomy predictions of friends, that it was not a mistake to seek a job that could become her "work." It was a choice—not a mistake. And, I'm happy to report, after six years and seeing her daughter through high school, Sunny F., is making a go of her true work.

What a tremendous release if we could relinquish the fear of making a wrong move, a mistake, and instead adopt the mind-set that chants, "I am making a choice for growth." No matter how that choice turns out, I am convinced of the tremendous benefit.

## Try It For Yourself

Take a personal incident which you now consider a "mistake", and imagine what it would be like if it had not occurred.

To do this, you might find it beneficial to try a stream-of-consciousness form of free-flow writing. Sit wherever you are most comfortable, with pencil and note-book on your lap. Now, taking deep breaths from the pit of your stomach, allow yourself to relax.

When you feel ready, let yourself write—without censorship—whatever comes up for you as you ask yourself, "What would my life be like now if I had not...?

Write out that scenario and how you feel about it. Make sure you note what persons, things, events, and insights would no longer be present in this "new" choice.

I am confident that you will then release yourself from the fear of personal loss through mistakes—because such choices ultimately bring benefit with them. Besides, some choices just have to be tried. What is worse than not succeeding is to spend the rest of your life wondering if you should have made a certain move and wishing you had.

I used this method of free-flow writing as a means to get some insight into what would often be called a "mistake"—a marriage that ended in divorce. Yes, I wrote about the pain, the confusion, the anger, and the loneliness. I wrote about how I felt like a nobody because my husband didn't want to turn over and hug me at night. "I'll mess my hair," he said. I felt about as desirable as a pimple between your eyes on prom night.

But, once I got through those feelings, I discovered how much that marriage brought into my life. I realized how much I learned about myself, how many wonderful, significant people are now in my life, even how a new profession and life blossomed because of that so-called "mistake." Yes, I'd do it all again, pain and all. Tremendous good bubbled over.

Great discoveries have also come from so-called mistakes. Some of our wonders of modern science have come because someone made an error, did something that was wrong. What do you know? Voila! A new enzyme. A new cure. A break-through.

I encourage you to allow yourself such a breakthrough. Take a respite and ask yourself if any of these attitudes might prohibit you from looking more deeply into your "work," job, and life.

As you continue to read the following chapters, become conscious if any of these attitudes begin to wave a warning flag. Listen and see if an attitude talks to you, trying to convince you that you couldn't possibly make such choices. Maybe you hear the voice of a parent or a relative.

Then ask yourself if you wish to listen to that voice or attempt to risk. The most important voice to hear is your own. It might be the one which hasn't gotten a word in edgewise for years.

This is all well and good but....

What if you feel too hopeless or helpless where you are right now to even consider a change?

What if you've made too many changes, only to find that the euphoric honeymoon of each new job gets shorter and shorter?

What if current financial demands seem to require that you stay put in a place where you feel put upon?

What if your organization is one of the many which has flattened out the pyramid for upward mobility—the only immediate key you see to salvation?

What if you are in the place where you have always wanted to be but find yourself inundated with the same problems you thought you had left behind?

What if you don't really know what you want and find yourself saying, "Hey, what can you expect? It's a job."

Does this mean that once again you must postpone happiness while waiting for the company to change, the boss to be transferred, the perfect work choice to be made, the proverbial ship to come in, the rules to be altered, the work load to be lessened, or the highest degree to be conferred?

No. No. No.

We do terrible mischief to ourselves by not learning how to flow with our current work experience rather than fight it or flee from it as our first recourse. To explain a little further, assume that your "gift," your dream work, is sitting on a rock ten miles downstream from a terrible stretch of white water. If you've ever run a river, you know that moving outside the tongue of the water (which looks as if it is attached to the very throat of the rapids) can very likely smash your craft against boulders. Portage around the boiling spot can throw you into dense thickets and impassable rock walls and is only considered as a final measure. You don't wait for some thundercloud to flood the river and raise the water table. Instead you deliberately, powerfully, steer into the rough water and after a few seconds' soaking, emerge at the end into a calm stream.

So too in your life. You must not wait. You'll make better, faster, more authentic progress to your dreams if you move from a sense of power and personal control over where you are right now! You might even find that you ARE in the right place to begin with.

The purpose of this book is to provide immediate help for today, wherever you find yourself. Using real-life examples, exercises, and researched methods, you'll discover ways to transform the ordinary into the extraordinary, to take charge of your response to the job environment—in short, to make work "work" for you AND to create a daily program for remaining connected to the rest of your life.

Self-mastery of what is, generates the fuel to move toward what can be.

There is one small thing which can stand in the way of being able to master and move from what "is" to what "can be"—the napping mind. Think about it this way:

You're driving down a road when all at once you realize that you have gone beyond your destination. Your mind was off on another channel and you have simply been going through the motions of driving. Startled, you look around, get your bearings, and try to figure out an alternative route. (You might also blame a passenger for distracting you.) What a frightening experience when you realize how much mechanical power was in your hands while you were oblivious to what was going on.

The same thing is true in our everyday lives. We move in and out of consciousness, unaware of the power we hold to alter our course. Too often, it's a traumatic event which snaps us into the here and now. May I suggest that you take your time with this book and fine tune your mental antennae to who you are, what you're presently doing, how you're behaving, and what might be done differently to allow you to live this day; stop blaming the passenger, and get on with the higher task of finding and becoming who you really want to be.

Lastly, in order to re-examine, reclaim, renew, and rejoice with this new-found sense of control in your work, remember the words of Sam Keen: "If what you see is what you get, then first you must change your eyes."

Let us look together at our work.

## Some Recommendations For Reading this Book

I've arranged the following chapters according to the steps of the work/life evalua-tion process which appear to unfold in our lives. The word "steps" is important.

Although some might occur simultaneously or possibly with years in between, to skip a step seems to result in imbalance. For example, we've first got to recognize what our symptoms of discontent are. We must explore our talents, needs, and feelings before we can make decisions to act on potential solutions. We must determine what "living" means to us so that our "job" or "work" choices are compatible. And once a choice is made, it is wise to know what to expect in the way of ups and downs, risks and rewards.

Let's begin that deeper look.

## Summary

1. A "job" is what you do for a paycheck. "Work" is what you do for a life.

2. Work is that significant, energizing activity which provides meaning to life. The ultimate task is to make "work" and "job" synonymous.

3. You might have to accept a "job" until you find your "work." You might keep a "job" to support your "work." But at all times, self-leadership is the key to sustainable living.

4. We have absolute control over everything in our lives because we have the power to choose. We choose our attitudes, how we feel about our "job," how we define "living." We can choose to strive for integration. We can choose to fully live.

5. Some attitudes that might hinder us from honestly looking at our work or job are:

    - I cannot waste what I was educated to do.

    - To be a success, I must make a lot of money.

    - To be a good person, I can't make too much money because money is evil.

    - I'm no good if I make a mistake.

6. Most decisions are not "mistakes" but rather choices for growth.

7. If you are not in a place to "change," consider actions which can lead to feeling in control.

*The great tragedy of our lives is that the major question of our existence is never put BY us—it is put by personal and social impulsiveness FOR us. Especially is this true in today's materialist, objectifying, authoritarian society, which couldn't care less about a person answering for himself the main question of life: "What is my unique gift, my authentic talent?"*

*As the great Carlyle saw, this is the main problem of a life, the only genuine problem, the one that should bother and preoccupy us all through the early years of our struggle for identity; all through the early years when we are tempted to solve the problem of our identity by taking the expedient that our parents, the corporation, the nation offer us; and it is the one that does bother many of us in middle and later years when we pass everything in review to see if we really had discovered it when we thought we did.*

*The way things are set up we are rewarded, so to speak, for NOT finding our authentic talent. The result is that most of our life is in large part a rationalization of our failure to find out who we really are, what our basic strength is, what thing it is that we were meant to work upon the world. The question of what one's talent is must always be related to how he works it on the world.*

*– E. Becker, The Birth and Death of Meaning (New York: Free Press—paperback, 1971)*

---

# Chapter Three
# When You're Stuck In the Mud

---

*How to turn from Frog to Prince (or princess)*

*— "Krrribitt"*

---

You wouldn't have picked up this book unless you were in a situation which seemed to be getting the better of you. You might be looking at alternatives, but somehow all your mental ability seems to be caught up thrashing over the work setting in which you find yourself. You need some answers, or at least some clues, as to why others seem to be enjoying and thriving in their occupations while you are feeling frustrated, maybe angry, bored, fatigued, unmotivated and spending energy getting nowhere.

"It's not fair," you mutter to yourself. "I just need a break like those other folks...."

"If only this company were larger (or smaller)...."

"If my job description were different...."

"If there were only more excitement and challenge in what I am doing...."

"If I could just have that one bread-and-butter client...."

"If the company would appreciate the hard work I do...."

"If only there wasn't so much paperwork and so many meetings...."

"If I didn't have to deal with so many unreasonable people...."

"If the kids were through college and I could go out on my own...."

"If I were paid more money...."

And on and on goes the internal, infernal chatter which seems to merely stress just how much you need to be someplace else and someone else.

After all, those folks who appear to enjoy their work pretty much all the time must be blessed with the ideal job. It is as if, by magic, the Wizard of Hogwarts had waved his star-spangled wand and transformed those wart-covered positions into tasks fit for royalty and, in the process, changed them from feeling like hop toads into members of the royal family.

And in a way, the analogy is correct. Except that the magic is not in the nature of the work but rather in the worker. They are wizards in their own right, capable of transforming coal into diamonds—for diamonds are nothing more than black lumps which stuck to their business under pressure.

That's not to say these magicians aren't making tracks for moving into other arenas... for finding that dream work which represents their special gift and talent. However, by learning how to take control and respond positively to whatever the job situation dishes out, they have energy left over to stretch, grow, risk, and glow.

To give you an idea as to how differently a prince (princess) and a frog operate in the world of the gainfully employed, let's look at some real-life examples.

I think we begin to get a picture of ourselves when we start to identify with others. For this reason, I have paired the case studies as closely as possible to their occupations. Discover how each one responds to what is currently going on in the work environment. See if you can identify what parts within the job description seem, at face value, to create the frog factor.

Also note your reactions when you first think of each person's line of work. Consider just how much excitement, reward, recognition, income, and satisfaction we stereotypically assign to that job title—all qualities which we arbitrarily think of as the "ideal" job.

And here's our cast:

Steve M., door-to-door sales representative of cleaning products, who literally walked into my life.

It was about 6:30 one evening when the door to my office opened and a merry voice hollered out, "I'm here to solve your cleaning problems!"

Startled, I raced to the reception desk, only to find a thin young man with a squirt bottle, rag, and a grin that stretched his mouth as wide as a Frisbee.

"That's right. This is the product you've been waiting for. My name is Stevie ... now just watch."

Too amused to disobey, I watched in amazement as he raced from carpet to wall to window, squirting and wiping, squirting and wiping.

"Now, isn't that something. It's non-toxic." (He opened the bottle and drank some of the fluid.) "And it's odorless." (He stuck the bottle under my nose.)

Interested, I began asking him questions—not only about the product but, more importantly, about himself. No, this wasn't his dream job. He had a degree in broadcasting from Temple University in Philadelphia. His real love was radio and the life of a disc jockey. Gab was his gift.

"I'm going to own a radio station one day. It costs $1.5 million, and this job is going to help me get it. Next month, I'll cut back on the time and begin to rep labels from musicians. But these four years have led me from Philadelphia to Los Angeles. No ma'am, it's been good."

With that, he tapped out a beat on the counter of the secretary's desk and began jiving out a jingle about dirt, spots, and his product.

"Don't tell me they taught you that song, too?"

"Oh no, ma'am. That was my way to keep from getting bored when I learned all the spots this stuff worked on."

He left with money is his pocket.

•••

*George S. (fictitious name), a postal carrier in a small, historic business community.*

The new tenant of an upstairs office in a two-story building couldn't figure out why his mail had not been picked up in a week. After all, he had seen the postal truck in the parking lot, but no carrier.

Then one day, while talking with the occupants of another office, postal clerk George walked in. A tall, well-proportioned man probably in his late twenties, George just stared at the newcomer, who introduced himself and asked about mail delivery.

"I hate having to walk up stairs," George grumbled. "Do you see all the build-ings on this route?"

The newcomer glanced down the street at the single- and two-story buildings now restored to the days of Spanish simplicity and balconied charm. "Aren't you glad this isn't New York!"

"Well, how would you like to deliver this stuff?" The carrier waved an advertisement tabloid. "This is just junk."

"I don't care what you think is junk. I want my mail delivered and picked up like everybody else."

The carrier shrugged his shoulders, pushed his wire-rimmed glasses back on his nose, and left.

"What a miserable character," commented the tenant.

•••

**Question:** Is there any problem picking out the frog from the prince? Stevie sees possibilities, takes charge for turning routine into fun. George views the primary task of being a mail carrier as a burden. Interestingly enough, George has held his job for quite some time with misery as company.

•••

*Ives R. (fictitious name), head of licensing for a multi-million-dollar entertainment conglomerate.*

Clouds of smoke part like the Red Sea when entering Ives' office. T-shirts, stuffed animals, toys, and games are scattered around the room—remnants of a job well done in turning a film character into marketable products.

Ives breathes a sigh. "Well, I'm as happy as I could be working. There's just too much to do. I'm surrounded by incompetent people. And I get sick of haggling over the numbers with potential vendors. But, they pay me too much money to leave."

•••

*Harry M. (fictitious name), chief executive of a prominent shopping center development company.*

At age sixty-two, two books of poetry under his belt and a list of civic commitments which would tax the energy of a pint-sized atomic bomb, Harry's eyes sparkle when he talks about his four children, his wife, the art world, and his upcoming shopping center projects.

"We've taken this one mall and turned it into a focal point for the community with an amazing array of customer services: uniformed hostesses to answer shoppers' questions, pet-sitting services, free wheelchairs, specially designed baby strollers, and free baby-sitting services. We look at each new project as a chance to be creative."

He admits that it's not easy. Dealing with city officials, community concerns, a fluctuating economy, and lawyers are part of the necessary headaches.

"But I even relish that. I look at each interaction as an opportunity to learn something about the other person, to see how creative I can be so that everybody wins in the process. Sure I get frustrated. But that's all part of the territory."

●●●

**Question:** How do frogs and princes view their interactions with other people? Who takes lemons and makes lemonade?

●●●

In 1981, career guru Richard Bolles read a story about a checker in a supermarket and later shared the tale in his newsletter. Although much time has passed, this princess's magic still carries a vivid example of alchemy at work.

*Barbara (fictitious name), supermarket checker.*

It's a job that few people would enjoy even a fraction of the time, and yet super-market checker Barbara has transformed the act of making the turntable start the food toward her: she does a little two-step, during which she causes her hips to hit the little bar that moves the turntable.

'Just wiggle your hips and the stuff keeps coming at you,' she says laughingly.

She has transformed the picking up of the cans and things: she tries to see how fast she can make them move. She has transformed the racking up of the mer-chandise on the cash register: she gets a rhythm going, much like a musician would. She has transformed the bagging of the merchandise: she sees it as a puzzle, trying to fit the pieces the best way possible within the bag. She has also transformed the dealing with the customers: she notes those with lonely faces, admires something they have on or otherwise fusses over them a little. She notes the children and brings in cookies she has baked at home to share with them when they come through her line. She responds in different ways to each cus-tomer, reserving her warmest response for the 'customer who treats me like a human being, not like a robot back here.'

She is given a job as a checker, but she becomes a dancer, a racer, a musician, a puzzle-solver, a counselor, and a Santa Claus. A fifty-six-year-old one, at that.

Pretty powerful picture. Particularly when contrasted with a checker I observed last week while standing in line. The checker said not a word to customers except "paper or plastic bags." An elderly customer, her wrist wrapped in an Ace bandage, struggled to lift the items from her cart to the counter. Rolling his eyes heavenward, the clerk folded his arms, gave a how-can-you-be-so-slow sigh, and made no move to help. Sure, the customer behind the woman quickly moved to her aid and the clerk proceeded—without comment—to ring up the groceries. But the checker's obvious job unhappiness sent a blast of cold air down the line.

•••

**Question:** Who controls responses to the situation? Do frogs or princesses think in terms of other people? Who likes to turn work into play?

•••

*Bill (no-last-name), the cook for a rescue mission in the Southern California desert.*

On Thanksgiving Day, the line around the mission bulged like the proverbial python, stuffed with humanity dressed in everything from unwashed rags to the humble dignity of a coat two sizes too small and a spotted tie for the holiday occasion.

Inside, Bill, a wiry little man (Popeye's double in starched whites) heaved a cauldron of giblet gravy to the back gas burner. He grinned at the volunteers, showing red gums around his two remaining teeth.

"Tell 'em they can come in now. We're ready to start dishing it out."

Amazingly, the small kitchen with its dented pots and pans and borrowed utensils spewed out ample food that day for some four-hundred folks, while Bill presided over the scene like a benevolent gnome. He'd been up for two days, cooking turkeys, making stuffing, cutting potatoes, and baking pies. Yet on "The Day," all traces of chaos had vanished.

"You see, there's a secret to all of this. You just have to plan ahead, be orderly, take it one step at a time, and it all fits in." He paused to banter a call from one of the mission regulars.

"I cooked in the Navy [no wonder he looked like Popeye] and always thought I'd like to try it full-time. 'Sides, it's regular and I've got control of this little space. It's mine. 'Sides, they like my cooking."

•••

*Susan R. (fictitious name), accountant for a community clinic.*

To enter Susan's office, one treads carefully. Stacks of invoices cover her desk and file folders are thrown around in disarray. The remnants of yesterday's lunch break are on a file cabinet and miscellaneous paper piles occupy other parts of the floor space.

"I just can't tell you how much work I am expected to do. It's driving me crazy." She puts her head in her hands and begins to cry.

"I feel so uptight about all of this. I'm also supposed to write policy on money procedures and yet I can't get the paperwork done. Nobody understands how hard I work. It's so hopeless."

•••

**Question:** Who begins to control the environment? Who takes control one step at a time?

•••

Jane H., president of a customer-service research and training organization.

Her soft accent breaking through the noise of the luncheon meeting, Jane talks with pride about her company.

"We have three hundred 'mystery shoppers' who work for us, and they do such a super job. That's what customer service is all about anyway—treating people like you'd want to be treated. We work with our employees, train them, and help them perform. I have the best partner and people to work with. We just take care of each other and do good work."

She paused for a minute and added in a whisper, "Why, we're looking at doing one million in business this year."

•••

*Priscilla P. (composite), president and owner of a prominent advertising firm.*

She sips her Perrier and shakes her head. "Good help is so hard to find. You think you've found someone and bingo! He makes mistakes; she wants to go home at five o'clock, or else I'm just not sure that I can trust them."

She admits to having a temper but insists that it is necessary when her name is attached to the business.

"And can you imagine this?" She leans forward and whispers. "The other day, one of my account executives and I were in a meeting and my employee yawned! Right there—in front of the client. That's just not acceptable!"

•••

**Question:** How does real royalty regard their subjects? Who sees human beings as potentially positive or potentially dangerous? Who lives the more peaceful life?

## What Does It All Mean?

Standing aside and looking at the actions of others gives us a pretty good insight into just what 'they" are doing wrong. It's certainly easier to see the freckle on someone else's cheek than the wart on our own nose. It's rather like the biblical injunction to stop pointing out the splinter in a neighbor's eye before we take the log out of ours.

The ability to take control over wherever you find yourself in the world of work requires honest, candid personal evaluation. It means critically looking at the activating agent which seems to push those out-of-control, miserable buttons. Then, and only then, can you begin to assess what might be done to alter the results you're experiencing.

But the first step is locating the activating agent. Once you've isolated just what keeps work from working for you, you can begin a process of determining just what you can do to get control back.

Let's be honest. The chance of finding your perfect work—with everything exactly as you want it—has about the same odds as you finding another Hope diamond. What makes the difference between the frog and the prince is how much attention each pays to the not-so-wonderful aspects of work. It reminds me of the old rhyme: "Two men looked out from prison bars. One saw mud. The other saw stars."

Did you also notice that the job description, title, and imagined salary of the various case studies didn't seem to make a difference in whether or not someone was happy. What made the difference was how each chose to respond to the situation.

## Activating Agents: The Potion Which Makes a Frog or Prince(ess)

If you are going to gain some control back in your life and handle the reality around you, then it is necessary to get a clear picture of exactly what you respond to (and how) which keeps the job or the work from working for you.

At this stage, we're not concerned about whether the activating agent has the force of a major hurricane or a weak tropical disturbance. Besides, as long as it is significant to you, it IS big. Later on, when you've regained some control, you might discover that the hurricane is diminished to a spring shower.

In the following section, see if you can identify what seems true for you. The lines after the questions are there in case you would like to jot down some thoughts which come to mind. Often, putting things in writing begins to clarify issues and areas for us.

## Activating Agent #1: Going Through the Motions

The words that best describe this category are: routine, little challenge, repetitive tasks, no sense of accomplishment, boredom, no sense of purpose or meaning.

The reality is that all tasks, no matter how exciting they are in the beginning, have a way of becoming routine. Don't we all know some people in glamour jobs and when we oooh and ahhh about what they do, they look at us blankly. What seems so marvelous to us has become as exciting as day-old socks for them.

I think the greater heroes are those folks, like the dancing supermarket checker, who can take a job which is routine from the very start and give it life and meaning.

# Questions:

(1) Is there an activity right now that has become routine and dull? What is it? Would you like to change it? What could you do? Alter, amend? How could you make it into a "game". And a critical question: does it really HAVE to be done? Maybe it no longer adds value but is done, "because we've always done it this way."

_____

_____

_____

_____

(2) What provides you with a sense of accomplishment? Do you have clear, written, measurable goals for yourself so that you can track progress or accomplishment?

_____

_____

_____

_____

(3) When was the last time you read, heard, or studied something new about your work? What area of your work do you feel you could learn more about?

_____

_____

_____

_____

(4) What activity outside of work gives you a sense of accomplishment? When was the last time you did that activity and how did you reward yourself for its accomplishment?

_____

_____

_____

_____

An insight I have is: _____

_____

_____

_____

_____

_____

# Activating Agent #2: People Problems

Ah, people. Sometimes we might feel that the world would be much better off without a number of them. The reality is that changing work locations or companies does not always change the people problems. Likewise, if we learn to cope with a difficult person, we have just added that much more power into our bag of magic tricks.

Mary Ellen W. (fictitious name) was hired as the manager in a communications department.

The vice president changed instructions daily, praised Mary Ellen one day for an item, and the next day screamed at her for the very same thing.

Mary Ellen was forbidden to talk with other vice presidents and told that managers were not to be seen in the employee cafeteria. Although asked her opinion, Mary Ellen knew that whatever resulted, the vice president would take all credit and level all blame on the others.

The final straw came when Mary Ellen worked up courage to ask the vice president why the staff would be told one thing and then punished for it. The vice president literally yelled at Mary Ellen and told her to leave the office.

Since Mary Ellen's work was good, the vice president did not fire her, but rather chose the cold/silent treatment and warned the department secretaries that they were to have nothing to do with Mary Ellen other than the most minimal interaction. None of the other senior officers would take on this vice president, and there was no one whom she could go to for a hearing. She left work each day with headaches and earaches.

This is a true story. At first blush, it would appear that Mary Ellen should have hightailed it out of there. (The truth is that it is easier to change organizations than it is to change the organization.)

However, Mary Ellen also learned something else. She determined that she would not fall prey to the vice president's plans. Instead, if she could control her response to the vice president and play whatever game was required (as long as it was in sync with her ethics and integrity), Mary Ellen would leave if and when she was ready.

It worked. And four months later, when Mary Ellen turned in her resignation, the vice president asked her repeatedly to stay.

The point is this: if we can at least control our responses to the problem people in our work life, we stand a much greater chance of making work/job "work" for us.

There are also those people who consider their customers and clients to be "bothers." The difficult ones, the complainers, the know-it-alls, are often just thorns and nothing more. Besides, solving what "bothers" a client is the best way to earn a loyal following.

## Questions:

(1) In your current work status, who seems to be able to push those buttons which result in negative responses on your part? A manager, a peer, a client, a customer?

_____

_____

_____

_____

(2) What situation creates the negative interaction? What do they do?

_____

_____

_____

_____

(3) How do you choose to respond? Are you happy/content with that choice?

_____

_____

_____

(4) Could it be that the person had no idea of his impact on you? Is your expectation out of line?

_____

_____

_____

_____

(5) Ask yourself these questions: So what? Who cares? What difference does it make? You might be in for a new understanding.

_____

_____

_____

_____

(6) I believe that people are basically _____

_____

_____

_____

_____

An insight I have is _____

_____

_____

_____

# Activating Agent #3: Work Overload

One of the dilemmas in dealing with work overload is that it has the possibility of being either real or imagined. It is real when someone is literally breathing down our necks, stopwatch in one hand, mounds and pounds of work in the other, saying that "This must be done by...." It is imagined when we assume that it must all be done at a specific time, when we have not told the right people just what our situation is, or when our own sense of guilt or fear drives us forward.

Work overload, or the perception of overwork, is serious business because it wears one down to the point of exhaustion. May I also ask you to consider that overwork can be the product of competency, incompetence, family myth, strong personalities, and/or competitiveness.

## Competency

It's not hard to see how the competent person keeps getting more and more of the work. After all, if we're so good at what we do, why don't we just do more? And because we like to buy into and accept that image of "The Competent Person", it might be difficult for us to blow the whistle and hold up our hand.

It's one of my problems. I'm just the girl who can't say "no". It does my little ego good to hear a staff member in my professional association tell others that I always deliver when asked to take on a new assignment. I feel myself puff with pride. After all, there are 4,000 other people who could have been asked. I feel so "competent". Until... until I realize that I made a serious mistake. Other things slide and the quality of my work and life slides downward as the quantity of to-dos move up. My fault. My ego.

## Incompetence

When someone is given work which is beyond his/her capacity, it might also be difficult to admit that help is needed. And so you work very hard at just trying to keep up.

A woman approached me at a seminar with this problem. She was overworked, trying to take medical-court cases off a dictating machine. Not only did she not know medical terminology, but she also had never worked the equipment. She had never shared this information with her manager but was, instead, blaming her boss for the amount of work she had to do!

## Family Myth

Family myth blends with workload when we grow up thinking that "idle hands are the devil's workshop." Or another myth is, "We pull ourselves up by the bootstraps. We never ask for help." In the former, we're afraid of legitimate space to rest and breathe. In the latter, we dare not admit that, "more busy hands make light work."

## Strong Personalities

Strong personalities may exert pressure on us because we are afraid to stand up for ourselves or to let someone know that our endurance level is not the same as theirs.

When I am with a certain colleague, I feel like I am moving in slow motion. Her speed of wit and movement leaves me breathless. She also has the sleeping and eating requirement of a hummingbird. In order to work with her, we have to set some ground rules about what pace I can keep.

## Competition

The competitive spirit has not only entered our marketplace, but also the back-yard in which we work. Have you ever noticed that some people like to play the "who's busier than who" game? It's rather like seeing who can have the darkest bruise, the most painful headache, the biggest to-do list.

There's an inherent feeling that the busier we are, the more important we must be. Alas, it's a trap that I fall into more times than I care to imagine.

# Questions:

(1) What is the work I am really supposed to be doing? Have I checked it out with others to see if I am on track? Am I over-doing the work, making it more difficult then it needs to be?

_____

_____

_____

_____

(2) Do I procrastinate so that there's too much to do in the allotted time? Do I try and get everything finished at once so I can have a clean desk and more work? Am I willing to say, "It is enough?" "Have I asked for help in prioritizing?" Remember, the only person who ever had all their work done by Friday was Robinson Crusoe!

_____

_____

_____

_____

(3) Do I compare myself with someone else and try to match his/her pace of work?

_____

_____

_____

_____

(4) Do I use the size of my to-do list as a measure of my importance?

_____

_____

_____

_____

An insight I have is _____

_____

_____

_____

## Activating Agent #4: The Environment

Much has been written about everything from noise to room colors as being potential causes for unpleasant work environments. However, when it comes to individual responsibility, I'm really talking about the actual space we work in—be it an office, a cubicle, even a car. One woman, unhappy with her work, discovered that as a traveling sales executive, what she really wanted was a desk. She rearranged her car space, put in some creative space-savers in the trunk, and voila! Satisfaction.

In the case of Bill's kitchen versus Susan's accounting office, one can see that the environment created a feeling of either control or disaster.

# Questions:

(1) How would you characterize your current work environment? What can you change? What might you be able to alter further if you think creatively?

_____

_____

_____

(2) Do your work space and materials provide a source of reassurance or dismay? What might make the difference?

_____

_____

_____

(3) Do you find yourself losing time trying to find things? Have you considered what outside assistance (a professional organizer) or what software (like Paper Tiger™) might help you?

_____

_____

_____

An insight I have is _____

_____

_____

_____

# Activating Agent #5:
## The Morass of Minutiae

Some people get most of their exercise running up mole hills—getting all steamed up before they ever find out what's cooking. In short, letting the trivial few become the gargantuan great.

This is a hard activating agent to honestly evaluate because it calls on us to admit that tiny things can drive us crazy.

## Questions:

(1) Are there any annoying habits of people whom you work with that bother you? What are those habits? WHY do they bother you? In the scheme of things, are they important?

_____

_____

_____

_____

(2) If you could change anything about your work, what would it be? Which would you do first? The primary items to change—are they major or minutiae?

_____

_____

_____

_____

An insight I have is _____

_____

_____

_____

# Activating Agent #6:
# Hidden Persuaders and Other Baddies

If you thought minutiae was hard, you haven't seen anything yet. This activating agent refers to our beliefs and attitudes about ourselves, our work, and people. And since we're here to discover frog factors so that you can begin to acquire the magic of transformation, we're looking at internal attitudes which can hamper us in taking control over where we are now in our lives and letting our work/job "work" for us.

Frankly, I don't know an easy quiz which can instantly produce a clear picture of less-than-optimum attitudes. Nor are there pat answers for overcoming and controlling such hidden persuaders. At best, it seems that if we can begin to uncover and acknowledge powerless attitudes as we become aware of them—or as other people point them out to us—then we stand a chance of changing those attitudes one at a time.

One of the more dangerous hidden persuaders that keeps us feeling helpless and hopeless is a fixed view.

A fixed view is a singular way of seeing something, the proverbial tunnel vision, the one way of interpreting data which says "This is the truth." There are always at least two options. Always. If I can't change what is, at least I can change how I choose to respond to it. Even no decision is a decision.

Fixed views get us into trouble when we hear ourselves saying things like "there is only one thing to do," or "this is the way I am; take it or leave it."

Fixed views can prompt us into doing nothing. "I can't ask for that. They'll say 'No.'" "I better not do such-and-such because this might happen."

The other attitude which also seems pervasive in situations in which we feel like frogs rather than nobility is a habitual pattern of looking for what is negative. We find everything that is wrong with a situation rather than what is right. And our attention focuses on loss rather than gain.

It is said that we teach what we need to learn. I admit to you that I am a learner in overcoming these hidden persuaders.

# Questions:

(1) Do you find yourself saying things like: "It can't be done"; "That's a stupid idea"; "What will other people say"; "Who am I to even consider that?"

_____

_____

_____

_____

(2) Do you find yourself saying things like: "But what will happen if"; "If only I would have"; "I'm just not worthy of any better."

_____

_____

_____

_____

(3) Do you punish yourself if you try something and it doesn't work, rather than applauding your efforts for making the attempt?

_____

_____

_____

_____

An insight I have is _____

_____

_____

_____

# The Wizard's Apprentice – Basic Magic #101

Having sat in the Magic Castle's room for the "close-at-hand" acts, I've been astounded at the effortless manner in which magicians perform seemingly impossible feats. I'm at a loss to explain them, and I'm sorely tempted to beg one of them to show me "the secret."

Unfortunately, I also know that even if they were to give me a look at the mechanism involved in their magic, I would still not be able to replicate the trick. Only years of practice, patience, and perseverance have resulted in their skill.

That's a healthy analogy to take with us on this journey of making wherever we are in life "work" for us so that we can begin to move closer into living our dreams and using our gifts. There is no one-step abracadabra. By the same token, I also believe that the magic needed to transform our lives and our work is tucked away in all of us. It's not reserved for the peak performers but is available to all of us if we only take the time and effort to consider options and actions which, though small, can be powerful.

That's a key word, "actions." Let's get going.

## Summary

1. There is no ideal job. The magic is not in the work but in the worker.

2. What makes the difference between frogs and princes/princesses is not the task but where they choose to concentrate their energy.

3. In order to begin to get control over where we are in our work life so that we can move to what can be, it is necessary to identify frog factors—activating agents which create a sense of powerlessness.

4. The more-common activating agents are:

   - Going through the motions—routine, boredom, no challenge

   - People problems

   - Work overload

   - The environment

   - Hidden persuaders and other baddies.

# Chapter Four
# How To Recognize A Pit When You're In One

*Sometimes I wish I just had a summer job here.*
*– John F. Kennedy*
*(to students working in Washington)*

You should see me now. Seated before a computer keyboard in a friend's office, I am attempting to use her compatible software program. The computer part is easy. It's her scruffy, pumpkin-colored cat curled in my lap that makes reaching the keyboard so difficult. Crazy cat. I've tried countless times to remove him (or her) but Crazy Cat (C.C.) keeps coming back.

C.C. just can't be that comfortable. Every time I strike a key, its head bounces back and forth in the crook of my arm. The furry bottom slops over my thighs and its neck tilts perpendicularly to its spine. Yet Crazy Cat stays.

It strikes me that a number of us are much like my feline lap-warmer. We'll frequently stay in a job of dubious "comfort" either by preferring the pain of the position to the perceived agony of change or by convincing ourselves that this is the best we can expect.

Or there are those of us who resemble the restless tomcat I see prowling around my friend's garden. Antsy and nervous, this fellow can't seem to find whatever he's looking for anywhere. I have a feeling that if he could talk, he'd loudly complain about everyone and everything. No matter where he goes, nothing is ever right.

Tomcat is like those wandering folks who can't quite focus on what is wrong with a job and therefore, everything is wrong. And it is always someone else's fault and not theirs that (sigh!) jobs are always so unfair and life is a sketchy place with only crumbs of happiness.

To complete the analogy, I note a mechanical cat sitting on the book shelf. If I wind the toy up tight, it will run in circles, be the epitome of a perfect cat, and stop dead in its tracks when the metal spring is exhausted. (Sound like anyone you might know?)

Please understand that I'm not being cynical or snide. Somehow it's easier for us to think of the symptoms of others before we can apply them to ourselves. Hence the necessity of this chapter. A doctor would never look for the cause and possible treatment of illness without first getting a list of symptoms. Neither can we.

There's also an ulterior motive in this chapter. If you bought this book, you're already aware that something is not clicking within your work/life or else you're looking to make what is good even better. But if someone bought this book for you, there's a very good chance that your friend is seeing an unhappy situation in which you are knowingly or unknowingly involved. Perhaps the following stories of real people might trigger a simultaneous "Why, that's me!" reaction.

## The Difference Between A Pit and a Pothole

Learning to recognize the real symptoms of a pit—and not the more shallow lows of a pothole—is critical. Let me explain.

A pothole symbolizes those down times that are to be expected of ANY job or work: pressure deadlines on a project; a new routine; a change in management; the presence of tasks which just aren't our favorites; a difficult individual; etc. The nice thing about potholes is that it is relatively easy to get out of them. I can see over the rim into daylight. In fact, maybe I know the road so well, I even know when they're coming and can prepare for it. And I CAN climb out.

For example, I truly enjoy speaking before audiences, giving workshops and seminars, and facilitating group dynamics. However, to do those things, I must spend time marketing my services—a task which I consider a pothole—a necessary evil.

Prior to writing this book, I experienced another pothole. A client gave me six weeks to develop and write a proposal in answer to a government solicitation. Every day, seven days a week, twelve to seventeen hours a day, I labored. The end result was 752 pages plus the mental state of a zombie. A true pothole. But if I did this type of work as a standard practice (and there are companies which do nothing but write proposals with horrendous deadlines), then I know—for me —I'd be in a pit.

Potholes are generally those things which can be either tolerated, rearranged, or even removed. However, people like Mr. Tomcat, spend most of the time creating an imagined pit from potholes.

Case in point: at the conclusion of a workshop I had given on coping with difficult people, a secretary came up to me and gravely complained about how bad her boss and work were. Her complaint: the boss made changes after she gave him the final copy of letters. "And I have to redo letters so often. It drives me crazy."

Yes, the secretary was proficient with her software. She rarely had to stay past regular hours. Yes, she received overtime. She just didn't like typing something over.

See what I mean? In her mind, she had turned a pothole into a pit. Other than provide some advice for restructuring the letter-writing process and communicating with the boss in a problem-solving manner, I could only inwardly wonder why she was a secretary in the first place. That seemed to be the true issue.

But a pit—now that's real trouble. There's no blue sky, no way out. It's nothing that can be tolerated, rearranged, or removed. The symptoms range from helpless frustration and apathy to rage or tremendous effort with little results (much like Mechanical Cat). But across the board, there is a feeling (even if denied) of not being in control; of continually not being in balance. I stress continually because potholes can also throw us out of whack, but only temporarily.

## The Pit Process

When I was 6 years old, I got the mumps. Mother knew it as soon as I couldn't swallow a pickle. I probably ran a fever, definitely developed chipmunk cheeks, and enjoyed lying in bed and coloring. However, if I had gotten the mumps at age 35, the symptoms would have been more severe and the recovery less pleasant.

The symptoms of a pit will also vary as we grow it through our jobs or work. Depending upon where we are at this particular time in our lives, the pit will manifest itself in different forms. And there will be numerous pits with each stage of growth.

# A Word About The Case Studies

Experience is a great teacher. This book contains first-hand or composite accounts about the experiences of others, what worked, and what failed. In this chapter, the case studies detail symptoms, just symptoms. See how each person behaved, how he or she felt, and what other areas of life were impacted during this "pit" stage. Record any similarities you might feel. Remember, without isolating the symptoms, you won't be able to determine if a solution works.

# The Granddaddy Of Pits – Burnout

Ever since New York psychologist Dr. Herbert J. Freudenberger popularized the phrase "burn-out" in 1980, the term has become a catch-all for a host of discontents ranging from the workplace to the home front. Despite all the years that have passed since he coined the term, "burn-out" has not changed but rather intensified. Freudenberger was more than correct. Look at his definition:

Burn-out: To deplete oneself. To exhaust one's physical and mental resources. To wear oneself out by excessively striving to reach some unrealistic expectation imposed by one's self or by the values of society.

He further expanded this definition by calling burnout, "a state of fatigue or frustration brought about by devotion to a cause, a way of life, or relationship that failed to produce the expected rewards."

What we see in this definition is the high achiever, the perfectionist, the workaholic, the goal-oriented idealist who demands the optimum out of every experience and maybe everybody. In my mind, I also visualize the "burned-out" individual as someone who has become out of sync by devotion or monumental striving in doing the real or perceived "work" of their lives.

Freudenberger served as a perfect example. During the 1960s, he set up a free clinic in the East Village of New York City to help the dropping-out, young flower children. Beset by drugs, illness, lack of money, and fear, the youth streamed into his clinic.

After completing a full day at his regular practice, this kindly psychologist would rush to the free clinic and stay until the early morning hours. He became obsessed with making the clinic work. At home (when he was home), his family members were met with irritability and a short temper. His friends anxiously inquired about his health. He angrily denied their observations. The turning point came when, instead of packing to go on a Christmas vacation with his wife and children, Freudenberger fell sound asleep for two solid days!

Small wonder that from his personal experience with burnout caused by over-dedication to his true work and unrealistic self-expectations, Dr. Freudenberger became a leader in understanding this prevalent modern-day problem.

•••

*Janet E., assistant magazine publisher.*

Hired fresh out of college to serve as editor on an up-and-coming slick city magazine, Janet bent to the task with vigor. She accepted everything that came down the line: all editing, the art department, the cover story, even typesetting. She put in seventy hours a week, juggled a marriage, and within two years "the work was the same, but I wasn't. I felt used, had no confidence and little self-esteem. There was no acknowledgment of what I was doing. No reward. The publisher was into sales but not content. She'd jump up and down over a big ad sale but never read my articles. I had no feedback. I felt I was an editor taking little steps instead of a really good editor taking giant leaps."

Working harder wasn't doing the trick. Nor were the obsessive games of solitaire which she played at home rather than talk with her husband. She felt trapped financially.

"I was using my salary to surround myself with luxuries—to forget work. I was spending money to make money, as a substitute for what was missing in my daily routine."

Then one day, she heard a giant, bottom-of-the-soul sigh. "I looked around. There was no one there. It had come from me." Without telling her husband, she quit her job.

•••

*Dr. A. O'Donnell (fictitious name), radiologist, late 40s.*

Absolutely fascinating. There are no other words to describe Dr. O'Donnell. From photography, to literature, to music, to world events, Dr. O'Donnell can command any group with his experiences and knowledge. He is well-respected in his field, keeps up with every journal publication, and is part of a highly respected hospital that grows by leaps and bounds, However, no new radiologists are added to the business. The consortium does not want to dilute the income and Dr. O'Donnell has bills, many bills.

One work shift rolls into another. Perfection is demanded. Play is a forgotten word. So is the time spent with his wife. She questions his exhaustion, the tension, the strain. His response: "One cannot admit being on the edge." It is a conspiracy of silence among the doctors.

Seeking professional guidance in dealing with the stress is seen as a sign of weakness and instability. Energy must be spent to keep up the pretense of superhuman ability.

At last, friends and loved ones are pushed away. The relentless grind continues. Dr. O'Donnell literally disappears from the sight of anyone not immediately connected with the hospital.

## More About Burnout

In looking at these stories, we can isolate more subtle symptoms: fatigue, despondence, a rejection of others, an unwillingness to talk about feelings, a push to do more than what can reasonably be expected, the rejection of time for relaxation, a sense of helplessness, and certainly denial.

Try this little quiz and see how you fare. Don't spend more than 30 seconds on each question. Your initial reaction is normally the most accurate.

Think about the last six months and then rank each response on a scale of 1 (rarely true) to 5 (definitely true).

1. Do you tire more easily? Feel fatigued rather than energetic? **1 2 3 4 5**

2. Are people annoying you by telling you, "You don't look so good lately"?
   **1 2 3 4 5**

3. Are you working harder and harder and accomplishing less? **1 2 3 4 5**

4. Are you increasingly cynical and disenchanted? **1 2 3 4 5**

5. Are you often invaded by a sadness you can't explain? **1 2 3 4 5**

6. Are you forgetting appointments, deadlines, personal possessions? **1 2 3 4 5**

7. Are you increasingly irritable? More short-tempered? More disappointed in the people around you? **1 2 3 4 5**

8. Are you seeing close friends and family members less frequently? **1 2 3 4 5**

9. Are you too busy to do routine things like make phone calls, read reports or send out Christmas cards? **1 2 3 4 5**

10. Are you suffering from physical complaints? **1 2 3 4 5**

11. Do you feel disoriented when the activity of the day comes to a halt? **1 2 3 4 5**

12. Is joy elusive? **1 2 3 4 5**

13. Are you unable to laugh at a joke about yourself? **1 2 3 4 5**

14. Does sex seem like more trouble than it's worth? **1 2 3 4 5**

15. Do you have very little to say to people? **1 2 3 4 5**

## The Burnout Scale

**0-25**      You're doing fine.

**26-35**    There are things you should be watching.

**36-50**    You're a candidate.

**51-65**    You are burning out.

**Over 65**  You're in a dangerous place, threatening to your physical and mental well-being.

The number is but an approximate score. If it's high—good news: you've been given a marvelous "heads up" that you can do something about. Denial won't work anymore. And believe me, you are NOT alone.

The current work environment is rich in social, psychological, and political drivers that cause fatigue and can eventually lead to burnout. These include:

- Extended hours. A February 2004 article in Fast Company indicated that American workers clock more time on the job than workers in any other country in the world, some 500 hours a year more than the Germans and 250 hours more than the British. A 60- to 75-hour workweek is typical for leaders.

- The 24/7 environment in which technology has us connected all the time. E-mail is seductive and too often, e-mail stands for ENEMY (of our life).

- A lack of closure when the crisis du jour keeps cropping up.

- A lack of control in a resource-scare environment.

- Over-committing and a failure to say "no" for either reasons of guilt or fear.

## Beyond Burnout

An observation: One does not have to be a high-achiever, a relentless striver, or a potential burnout victim to be in the pits; to feel that life is out of control and tasteless. In short, one does not have to burn out before taking stock of the situation and figuring out corrective action.

It also seems to me that there are subtle distinctions as well as similarities between true burnouts and other "pits."

You'll see what I mean in the following case histories.

## The Empty-Feeling Pit

When we were kids and played hide-and-seek inside on rainy days, it was generally some object instead of one of us that hid. I can still hear the clues as we wandered around the living room: "Naw, you're cold. Better now. Getting warmer. Nope, cooled off. Now you're hot, getting hotter...."

Mother had another way of saying it. We were "in the right church but the wrong pew." So it is with the pit that comes from being "warm" in discovering your "work" or in handling your "job." You're in the right general area, but not quite there yet. There's discontent, anxiety, maybe even disappointment. Something just isn't right. At the place next to your heart, it seems very empty.

•••

*Robert W., psychotherapist.*

One brief conversation with Robert and you become very glad that his mother didn't triumph with dentistry. His bristly black beard contrasts against gentle blue eyes that crinkle with warmth when he listens and guides individuals through personal-life transitions. His talent is counseling; a gift that surely would have been lost on dental crowns and upper-bridge plates.

But it has taken Robert years of his own movement through pits to arrive at a place where his "work" fits and that empty feeling has been replaced by internal satisfaction and creative expression.

By 1970, with a masters' degree in psychiatric social work, Robert was well established in Beverly Hills as a psychotherapist and family counselor. The "pew" certainly looked right: XKE Jaguar; apartment with a prestigious address; married to a gorgeous therapist; enough clients to have a second home in Laguna Beach. But something was missing.

"We had been to enough charming dinner parties in homes with Spanish live-in maids to have tired of that. I looked at others in the profession who had larger houses, were chairmen of departments, had bigger practices, and I asked myself: "If I get to be them, will I be happy?" I got to see that none of those things would give me what I was looking for."

His significance in life seemed too shallow, without meaning. In spite of external signs of success, a feeling of incompleteness led him to continual searching. In the big picture, where and why did he belong?

•••

*Cheryl P., former director of communications of a professional association.*

Unlike many of us who just fell into our first occupations without any clear-cut purpose, Cheryl's earliest memories were of writing. "My mother still has the news clipping of some essay contest I won in first grade," she chuckled. "They probably printed every entry."

For the later-to-become reporter, it was her first of many newspaper clippings. But it would take the reoccurrence of pits and repeated attempts before she figured out just what form her writing career was to take.

It took seven years on the news and feature beats of two daily newspapers for the first round of symptoms. "The stories weren't interesting any more. Even the features didn't stimulate me. I was just plain bored. That's when I thought about going into public relations—something related to writing but a new world. But even though I interviewed with a firm, I still wasn't ready to give up my identity as a reporter. There's something very romantic about being a reporter. People look at you with such interest. It's a hard role to give up."

But a year later, the boredom had doubled and cynicism crept in. "Sluggish, unenthused—yes, that's how I felt. The challenge was gone for some reason. I'd find my mind drifting in interviews, wanting to sleep in city council meetings. I wasn't interested in what I was writing and neither, I discovered, were a lot of people.

And I wanted something positive. As a reporter you generally do look for the worst, for the bad news, and go in with that attitude. That was another aspect— reporters being objective. The longer I worked, the more I realized that they aren't and that's hard to live with. I could feel myself becoming cynical about both my personal and professional life."

A brief stint with a public-relations firm and Cheryl headed for executive ranks with the title of director of communications for a major medical association. Within three years, new symptoms were present.

"By the end of the first year, I started missing the writing. I got so involved in meetings that there was never time to write well. Between meetings and politics, I found I wasn't very comfortable. Something kept nagging at me, telling me 'You're unhappy because you're not writing. That's what you enjoy most.'

"I hated to go into work. I hated the pressure of knowing that I now had a mortgage payment over my head. There was a bad bout with the flu and my throat had a feeling of tightness which the doctor said was related to the autonomic nervous system. I could swallow fine but there was this sensation. In one sense, I was relieved when the doctor said it was stress. But in the other sense I felt helpless. And my stomach aches seemed to grow each day I was there. I just felt that I really wasn't doing what maybe I was best at. I could do whatever they gave me to do, but I wasn't enjoying it. And I didn't like managing people at all."

## The End-Of-The-Road Pit

There's another form of pit which comes when you are faced with the fact that you're probably not even in the right "church," let alone pew. You've done it all, accomplished whatever the task was (maybe with much success), and a long path of nothingness faces you in the night. There is no opportunity for moving up or down, only out. The empty feeling next to your heart is also accompanied by an ache at the base of your spine.

The base of your spine is considered to be the location for the energy to bring things into reality, to create, to give life. When the ache is centered there, confusion, dismay and maybe even despair can seem overwhelming. There's a sense of having nothing to show for the effort expended.

•••

*George G. (fictitious name), recently retired senior executive for a multinational corporation.*

George learned that birthrights can be dangerous things. At least so it seems to George, an impressive silver-haired gentleman whose good looks knock years off his age and belie the fact that he grew up during the Great Depression.

Coming from an era when job security meant sticking with one company until you accepted a plaque and a Rolex watch. George's story is brief but poignant. From a journalism degree, he entered his uncle's company and rose to become vice president of public relations, advertising, and industrial relations. But at the beginning of his second decade with the firm, he quit. The dilemma: personal worthiness.

"By materialistic standards, I had it made. But I felt unappreciated. My career had peaked. And I doubted my ability. Did I get where I was because of the good fairy who made me or was I competent? I was anxious, depressed. My marriage was falling apart, even though its demise didn't happen for another ten years. But most of all, I felt it would really die if I didn't do something."

•••

*Gary R., former executive in the recording industry.*

At the time Gary encountered his most significant pit, this middle-aged father of two teenaged daughters had come quite a long way for a high-school dropout from Brooklyn. His accounting degree earned in night school and his quick understanding of the music industry pushed Gary up the ladder of the recording business. Almost each career decision had been made with wisdom and good timing. But now, earning six figures as an executive for a national trade publication for the recording industry, the end-of-the-road pit appeared.

With the company moving its headquarters from California to New York, the job as director of business affairs was changing. Budgetary functions, licensing agreements, departmental liaisons were gone. Life became routine. "Every day became less challenging, less enjoyable, less exciting. I was more involved in handling the company's conventions, but it wasn't enough to fill the void. I felt trapped, frustrated, angry, upset, annoyed. The promised new publication and attendant challenges did not appear. What was the way out?"

Gary wasn't even sure he wanted to remain in the industry which had pleased him for so long.

•••

*Charles D., former president of a marketing corporation.*

Well over twenty years ago, Charles entered the infant home-improvement industry with his ideas for marketing and sales just tumbling around in creative juices. It only took eight years in the corporate world to convince this young executive that the grass was greener in his own back yard. "So I started a marketing company for the industry, representing manufacturers and retailers, training store people, warehousing goods, and developing merchandising techniques."

Within ten years, the company had grown from nothing to around $6 million in yearly revenue. But Charles was antsy, ill-at-ease. "I lost interest in the business. Started dabbling in psychology classes at night. I really didn't have anything planned beyond my company. And so I plodded along, half-hearted. The company kept growing. The decision of what to do with my work got more difficult. We had a nice big building, an impressive office. I was like a king holding court. But it wasn't doing it for me. I thought of ways to phase down, to go part time, to ask my partner to run the company, but nothing worked.

There was no joy. Selling tool boxes to home-fixer-uppers just didn't do it for me. I was afraid to leave. So I spent three years trying to juggle reality, putting on a patch that wasn't working, trying to reconcile myself that it was really time to move on."

The role of a hotshot, high-powered company president was moving stage left.

## The I-Wanna-Be-Me Pit

Once you understand what is your "work" (i.e., that which excites and has meaning for you), the closer you come to being in a pit if you cannot perform that "work" as either an after-job activity or as part of the job. Assume you truly delight in working with people and in solving personnel problems and yet your job has you seated all day at a computer terminal. Because of a long commute, you're too tired at night to do anything but eat and sleep. Chances are you'll be feeling any or all of the symptoms mentioned in the other pits.

Note the difference between this and the Empty Pit. In the Empty Pit, you are doing what appears to be the meaningful work of your life and yet you want more. In the I-Wanna-Be-Me Pit, you are not getting to do that "work" at all.

## The Potpourri Pit

While the other "pits" have more individual character and symptoms and seem to require dramatic action, we also experience a state of non-living when we're out of balance for a multitude of reasons. It's the old trying-to-keep-seven-balls-in-the-air-at-once routine, probably compounded if you want a standing ovation for a perfect performance at the end.

●●●

*Ronda S., former language/speech and hearing specialist.*

With a gift for gab, a credential in communication disorders, and some bilingual skills in Spanish, Ronda delighted in her school position. But the pressure of a special-education environment with overwhelming paperwork left Ronda feeling constantly behind.

"I tried to restructure the situation by transferring to a year-round school to see if a regular break would relieve the stress. For the first few years that switch helped. With four vacations a year, I had a sense that I had four beginnings."

The school itself was exciting: There were high-powered professionals on staff, an innovative principal, a model program as a community school, child care for mothers, a foster-grandparent program, and a strong volunteer group. Still looking for more challenges, Ronda also volunteered for additional work at the district level. Although admittedly spread too thin, it took a divorce to really put the imbalance wheels in motion.

"I'm not extravagant, but without a second income I needed additional funds to stay in my California home. So for about a year, I worked after hours teaching six Japanese families. I'd find myself drained at the end of a day. I realized that from morning to night I was encouraging people to communicate. I had about twelve therapy groups, didn't take a full lunch, and then left the school to teach again. I was attempting to inspire people all day long. When I did get home, to keep up social contact with my friends, I'd spend hours on the phone. I was overwhelmed with communication."

She again attempted to alter her environment, cutting out phone calls, taking lunches, but the imbalance continued. Another pressure was added: romance. "After being single for nearly four years, I was involved in a crazy romance with someone living on the East Coast. We felt strongly about the relationship, so, once again, there were requirements—writing, planning trips, travel. He finally moved within some seventy-five miles of me, but then there were weekend commutes. I also sold my house and within six months I had moved three times.

By Christmas of that year, I realized I wasn't in control—working two jobs, commuting every weekend, not being committed to an exercise program. I had stomach pains, but the tests for an ulcer were negative. It wasn't just the work that was in the pits. It was everything!"

## The People Pit

Have you ever been invited as a first-time guest to a meeting, a party, or a dinner where you discovered that you weren't quite comfortable with the other people? Or do you remember, at least once in your education, a teacher whom you barely tolerated through a semester? The mix was like oil and water.

Just because we're now grown up (make that "growing up"), it doesn't mean that we won't encounter such groups or individuals in our work/job lives. In most cases, I believe such people are truly only "potholes" who can be handled, but, I also believe there are those few instances where the presence of an individual or a specific corporate culture can evoke all the symptoms of a pit: fatigue; anger; inability to work effectively; illness; despondency; even despair. It is brought on not by the everyday tasks at hand, but by human interaction.

•••

*Mary B. (fictitious name) industrial-relations director, "Big Board" corporation.*

Mary generally loved her work. When she could travel and do hands-on assistance at plants away from corporate headquarters, she shined. But daily work at the home office had become a trial by fire.

She answered directly to the vice president of communications, a man who insisted upon a rigid adherence to his personal management style, who took sole credit for any good idea generated from the department, and who would laugh one minute and then fly into rages and yell the next. Employees tiptoed around. Mary never knew which end was up. In her then-fifteen-year career, she had never encountered such behavior, nor such restraints.

Then one day Mary made the mistake of correcting the vice president. He flew into a rage and accused Mary of trying to sabotage the department. Mary left, gulping down the anger.

In the weeks to follow, the vice president coldly ignored her. The department secretary came in to tell Mary that the vice president had warned other employees to stay away from her. Mary was distraught. She'd go home in knots. There were constant headaches.

Mary had moved across the country to take the job and had no other area contacts. Corporate policy, as dictated by the vice president, prohibited her from joining professional organizations which met during the day. She felt trapped and alone.

## The Dimensions of Pits

Just as a fever can range anywhere above 98.6 degrees, so too can the symptoms of being in a pit vary in intensity. Some days are harder than others; some pits deeper than others. Some symptoms can be overcome in hours while others might take years. But the most important thing in beginning a journey of self-discovery and self-growth is the recognition that where you are now in your work life is not where you want to be.

I must hasten to add a postscript here. Some "pits" occur literally and figuratively overnight: job termination; bankruptcy; divorce; death of a spouse or a significant person. Because of the special trauma created by such tragedies, Chapter Six is reserved just for handling these cases. But regardless of why a pit is present, the same opportunity for personal growth and the same process of exploration apply.

Throughout the rest of the book, you'll discover what most of the aforementioned people as well as others did to understand and alter the current course of their lives.

# Summary

1. Too often we fail to acknowledge the symptoms of a pit or even a pothole because we are afraid to change.

2. Some people make pits out of potholes. A pothole is the to-be-expected negative side of any work or job. (I might love selling, but I hate filling out sales reports.)

3. A pothole can be tolerated, arranged, or even removed.

4. A pit is a mental and physical state of being which cannot be tolerated, which cannot be ignored, which has resulted in imbalance throughout all corners of your life.

5. Burnout, the pit of high achievers, perfectionists, and workaholics, is the exhaustion of one's energies brought about by striving to reach some unrealistic goal or by devotion to a way of life that fails to produce the expected reward.

6. One can be in a pit without having burned out.

7. The primary symptom of the Empty-Feeling Pit is exactly tha—a feeling of being "not filled" with enough of the chosen work.

8. The primary symptom of the End-of-the-Road Pit is a feeling of being lost and confused in determining what might be your "work."

9. The primary symptom of the I-Wanna-Be-Me Pit is frustration because there is no allowance for your "work" in any part of your life.

10. The Potpourri Pit is a collection of symptoms stemming from imbalance in multiple areas besides your work/job.

11. You might be in a pit with your current employment if you experience some of the following symptoms: constant fatigue; reluctance to go to work; lack of motivation; boredom; sadness; irritability (either at home or at your place of employment); increased use of alcohol, drugs, or cigarettes; despondency; despair; constant complaining; inability to laugh; illicit sex; crying jags; medical complaints (head, stomache, neck, back, throat); continual denial when asked if anything is wrong; forgetfulness; little time for play, for friends or self; and an unwillingness to share feelings.

# Chapter Five

# Okay, It's a Pit – Now What?

---

*If you do not change your direction,*
*you are likely to end up where you are headed.*

– Ancient Chinese Proverb

---

From the ruins of ancient civilization, archaeologists have uncovered human skulls with a small hole bored into the forehead. It is theorized that early surgeons sought to relieve migraine headaches by allowing the evil matter and/or demons to escape through the opening. Pretty drastic measure for someone suffering from a pounding cranium. But then, I guess, any action was preferred to pain. And there certainly was a change for the patient: a number even lived with new bone growing over the gaping hole!

I relate this tale to put the wisdom of the Orient into perspective. The proverb quoted in the beginning of this chapter rightfully implies that unless action is taken—unless a change is made—things will stay exactly as they are.

May I suggest that MANY changes are possible without resorting to radical surgery. You have more options than our hole-in-the-head ancestors. Those early neuro-surgeons performed the operations because they were aware of only one cause of the pain. In reality, there were many.

So too will there probably be a number of causes for the symptoms, the imbal-ance, the non-living feeling which we might encounter in our work/job lives. The purpose of this chapter is to provide guidance in helping you to determine just what might be some causes for the pit or imbalance as well as steps which various individuals have found helpful in exploring potential changes in direction.

# First Stage: Analysis Of Situation

Accept responsibility for your role in the pit.

In the second chapter, I listed four attitudes which could prevent someone from even beginning to look at work and life. To think that one is perpetually pro-grammed by an educational track, that success can only be defined by money (and the converse attitude that only the shallow can avidly seek riches), and that mistakes are taboo, are all limiting attitudes.

There are other attitudes derived from our perceptions of life which also create tiny, airless boxes into which we stuff our souls. The good news is that we have the power to burst out of these boxes.

However, what happens so easily is that we give away our power. Often, without even knowing it, we let others have control over what we do and how we feel. And then someone or something outside of us takes the blame.

At down times, the internal conversations with ourselves might go something like this:

"Okay, job—I'm miserable and it's your fault. You did it, not me."

"Boss, make me happy. You're responsible for knowing what I need."

"It's my wife's fault that I must work so hard. She wants expensive things."

"Everybody wants everything yesterday. If I'm going to keep this job, I have to please everyone."

"I'm too old to change. I hate what I'm doing but I can't give up my lifestyle."

Pretty powerless monologue. But it doesn't have to be. You helped create your situation and therefore you also have the power to re-create it. You are not a victim of circumstance. You are not helpless. But first you must determine just how you are contributing to the "pit."

## Response To Personal History

Each of us has his own mental scrapbook of experiences which can influence our choices in positive and negative ways. Remember the scene from "Gone With the Wind" when a starving Scarlett O'Hara frantically digs through the burned earth, finds a carrot and swears, "With God as my witness, I'll never be hungry again."?

From that point on, Scarlett's actions are predicated on the fact that she chooses to feel she never has enough. She always wants more clothes, money, food, admirers and therefore creates the situations to respond to that experience.

In real life, one might also give more power than is deserved to personal experiences.

When Dr. Freudenberger began examining the causes for his burnout, he realized that the very idea of a clinic for flower children came as a result of his exceedingly difficult childhood in Nazi Germany. He over-identified with the youth of the 1960s who elected to slip away from the norms of society. There was, in fact, little correlation between those young adults and the German youth who were pursued by the Gestapo and made homeless by a national holocaust.

•••

Another example:

*Susan, age 40 (composite), an attorney.*

Ever since passing the bar, she has successfully scratched and clawed her way through cases which few lawyers would have won. Although there has been little time for significant relationships, she always finds time to write home about each case, enclosing her news clippings as often as possible.

Her dad is thinking of retiring and expects Susan to come home to take over his legal practice. She can't put her finger on it, but lately she's been getting severe headaches and finding that she is almost too wound up to sleep. Friends seldom call her because she abruptly tells them "I have to go now. I'm too busy."

With the help of a counselor, Susan is beginning to realize how much she has allowed a personal experience to color her life, to create her pit by living out the life of a dead brother.

When she was 10 years old, her only brother died of leukemia. Her parents were devastated, particularly her father. He had often talked about the family law practice, which had been started back in the 1800s, and how Tommy would help carry on the tradition. After the funeral, her dad started to cry. She was crushed to see tears streaming down his face. From that moment on, Susan determined that her dad would never be hurt again.

Although she has enjoyed the practice of law, Susan now feels trapped by the thought of maintaining her practice in the family's small hometown. Furthermore, she has begun to feel alone and empty in her work—thus trying to work harder to make up for the loss.

Although not all personal history is as dramatic as the incidents above, I think the message is clear. We can't change direction until we decide just how much control we have allowed people or events to have over our lives. Yes, I agree with poet John Donne when he says, "I am a part of all that I have met." But this does not mean that who we are and what we do must be determined by forces outside of us. Flavored, yes. Cast in stone, no. That would make living reactive instead of pro-active.

## Response To Social Pressure

The common thread which runs through all pits is a feeling (even if denied) of being out of control or out of balance. Another cause for that feeling could be the fact that one is attempting to satisfy the collective wish of a group. Probably today's most prevalent social pressure comes from the movement of women into both higher and newer positions. Instead of the social pressure to be a contented housewife and mother, the push is for independence, status, and title.

Cheryl determined that her acceptance of such pressure was contributing to the pit. "I tried to convince myself that I should be an executive. That I had it made. Me, a director of communications. But that was someone else's expectation—not mine.

"I became aware that one of my inner struggles was trying to live up to the 'whole' woman—climb the ladder. But it wasn't me."

Another woman plugged away for over a decade as an urban planner before she wised up to the fact that her dissatisfaction came because all along she had wanted to be a teacher. But teaching had been stereotyped as a female profession, so she opted for a non-traditional role.

What counts most for living is not the status of upward mobility of our work/job, but rather our happiness. For both men and women, the pressure to be a "success" often overshadows "being happy."

# Response To Ethical Considerations

The question here is not what business you are in, but rather what business practices are involved. Interestingly enough, I have encountered cases where subjects were unaware that part of the intrinsic cause of their uncomfortable position was a personal conflict with the work they were called upon to do.

*Maureen C. (composite), accounts payable clerk for a prominent hotel.*

Every night, Maureen comes home just exhausted. It seems she is always behind in her work and that the most hated portion of her job is telling vendors that they must wait to be paid.

"The worse part is that I know what the owners take out of the business. They have a fancy house and just bought a limousine. Yet I have to keep inventing excuses because we're often months in arrears."

In her personal life, Maureen pays each bill as soon as it arrives in the mail. Yet her inability to control vendor payment creates a dilemma.

•••

*John W. (composite) sells circuit boards for an engineering company.*

John prides himself on answering all phone calls, following up on inquiries, and placing accurate orders. But once the orders hit the assembly process, he loses control of the client's order. Sometimes shipments are delayed or lost. John has promised the goods and feels personally responsible for the delinquent account. The company can't always deliver in the fashion he thinks is needed.

If a portion of John's personal sense of integrity is linked to the delivery of a product, then John must become very clear on how much control he needs, and if such control is ever even possible in a sales position. Without that understanding, one cause of John's pit will be unresolved.

# Response To Self-Image and Self-Esteem

Self-image is the picture you hold of yourself. Based upon that picture (which may be distorted), you take action. Remember Janet E., the assistant publisher? She felt incompetent and ill-equipped for her job. Her resultant action, which contributed to the burnout, was to assume more tasks than were humanly possible and to work a tremendous number of hours.

The hidden agenda behind some out-of-control workers is to imagine that longer hours, more duties, or heavier workloads will increase the depleted confidence or negative self-image. Until one comes to grips with the internal cause behind burnout, the scenario will be repeated from job, to job, to job.

Another dangerous self-image is that of the Hopeless Hannah or Helpless Howard. These are well-meaning folk who got the message early on that only "luck" or "getting a break" controls the world. And so they never ask for what they want. According to former career consultant Barbara Abrams Mintzer, the people who don't go out of the pit to seek the job/work they want are not only afraid of rejection, but they've already rejected themselves!

Self-esteem is the value you give yourself. The perfectionist, the relentless striver, the Wonder Woman and Superman frequently feel that unless work/job is done according to exterior signs of success, they have no personal worth. This might be compounded by a sense that no one can do it but them. Additionally, while they might exude confidence, their problem is multiplied by a self-image which demands only pinnacles and no plateaus. Omnipotence is a killer task master.

At face value, this might seem contradictory. True, we've established that our job or work is the primary source of personal identity and that "work" is that activity which puts meaning and energy into our lives. But, that does not imply our value, our worthiness as human beings, is determined by the success of our efforts.

Our work or job should never be the single determinant of self-esteem. Unless we separate our being from work, we will always be vulnerable to any professional setback, criticism or negative feedback.

## Determine Level of Expectations of Work/Job

Consider this reality testing. Ask yourself if what is expected of you (or what you expect of yourself) is reasonable. Remember, frequently the "pit" comes from over-dedication, over-exhaustion for a perfectly legitimate reason.

In Dr. Freudenberger's case, not only was it unreasonable to expect himself to work night and day, but the clinic was understaffed, the number of clients too great, the community support lacking.

Our other burnout victim, Dr. A. O'Donnell, was being called upon to attend patients without having sufficient opportunity to rest and regroup. Additionally, since his personal expectation is that he must also keep current with journals, whatever little time he has is spent in educational reading. Both the personal and professional expectations are severely tilted. When this is coupled with an abandonment of personal power to do anything but remain within the vicious cycle, the outlook is grim. Sad to report, until Dr. O'Donnell or someone else within that medical community cries "enough," the pit remains.

A word of caution. It's mighty easy to turn a pothole into a pit when it comes to expectations. Could it be that you are grinding yourself into a pit when, in fact, that is not what is expected of you at all? Have you created more burden for yourself than necessary? Or are you turning reasonable expectations into burdens because you don't quite belong in that role?

## Determine if the "Pit" Is Really Work/Job

Because we spend most of our waking moments in a place of employment, it is understandable that we are inclined to consider work as our central reason for non-living.

Work can be the scapegoat. In fact, it might be a good cover-up for what is the real root of unhappiness and a feeling of imbalance. I know. I did it. In my first real go-around with a pit, I considered the fact that I was bored, uncomfortable, unchallenged, and without joy as being solely the result of work. "That's it," I thought. "I need different work. I need challenge, something new."

Thankfully, somewhere between cleaning up my resume and beginning a cursory exploration program, I realized what was really wrong. I had no business doing anything else until I came to grips with my marriage. Only the resolution of the real cause for my pit allowed an authentic opportunity to seek work and balance.

Work or a job might also be the cover-up for a denial of health issues. The man who decides that chest pains, headaches, and mood swings are the result of work might really be carrying a time bomb inside that will go off regardless of where and how he works. While job stress and physical ailments can be symptoms of being in a pit, conversely such ailments can still be signs that something is indeed wrong physically. A chemical imbalance might be the root cause for an

70

individual going through several jobs, always finding the tasks too stressful and fatigue being a constant companion. Correct this imbalance and work becomes easier. The pit has been filled in.

One of the harder health issues to handle is alcoholism. Although massive efforts are underway to educate the public about this disease, the usual response of a sufferer is denial. The job becomes the cause of tension, depression, conflicts with fellow employees and managers, difficulty in handling the job responsibilities. In reality, the disease of alcoholism is the true culprit.

Once again, even in this step, introspection and the willingness to honestly look at our contribution to the "pit" becomes paramount.

## Take Action to Re-energize In Order to Analyze

It's impossible to even begin to assess what is happening when all your energy is gone, used up, or scattered. You must retouch, re-center yourself by creating a space in which you can think, in which you can remove yourself temporarily from the pit. By creating mental or physical distance, you regain at least some small measure of control.

Renewing yourself can be as simple an activity as taking a long, hot shower or a bubble bath or playing the piano. Chances are, if you are imbalanced, that activity will be something in which you have not indulged recently.

Here are but a few examples of renewing activities: silence, solitude, laughter, sleep, playful reading, music, prayer, good conversation with a sharing of feelings, dancing, exercise, arts and crafts, writing, or hiking ... whatever allows you to feel at least some semblance of calm ... whatever soothes your soul without altering your ability to thoughtfully experience and reflect.

I liken this step to the old Alka-Seltzer commercial—"plop, plop, fizz, fizz, oh, what a relief it is." Notice the word is "relief," not "cure." If possible, take whatever small steps will begin to give you some control so that you might look at the bigger picture and THEN begin to change direction. For example, individuals suffering from burnout might immediately reduce at least some level of workload. One might make an appointment with a counselor or a physician.

# Stage Two: Determine What Must Be Acted Upon First – And Do It!

Here's another example of first-things-first. From the People Pit, Mary B. realized the first thing that had to change was her reaction to the vice president's personality and management style. Certainly depression and headaches were going nowhere and Mary knew she was definitely not coping. She also admitted that unless she could internally handle a stressful person, she'd probably continue to encounter the same problem.

Mary spent a weekend just talking and listening and talking to herself. She reevaluated her work and decided, "Darn it, I'm good." She realized that her self-confidence had been diminished by the confrontations with the vice president.

By the end of the weekend, she felt that her self-esteem was back in place and understood, finally, that the vice president was an insecure, troubled manager. With that acknowledgment, Mary knew she could internally deflect the antagonism, and knowingly play the corporate game until she had time to analyze her next move.

In this example, Mary gained personal control but did not make a major decision. However, some pits require harder efforts to gain initial control and greater space for re-energizing.

•••

*Janet E., assistant publisher.*

"When I quit the magazine, I realized that it was not the work environment that had to be changed. It was me and how I reacted to it. I had been so insecure and eager to please."

Ironically, Janet began to regain her confidence when she realized that she herself had burnout, and queried Parade magazine about a feature article on the topic.

"When the check came from Parade for $1,500, I felt my writing was validated. It took two years and lots of paid writing assignments to convince myself I was competent."

"I went back to the magazine. Only this time, I came feeling like a winner. A mediator got us together and I was able to structure the job I wished. I don't manage so many people, I work more realistic hours, and I get the salary I want.

I also knew that the publisher would probably never change and read my work. So, in order to receive some of her enthusiasm and recognition, I now keep the tally of the sales records and present that to her each month."

From her two-year hiatus, Janet also was able to give up the feeling that she had to be perfect and always in control. "There's no more holding things inside. At work, when something is wrong, I now say, 'There's a problem, let's fix it.' I just love what I'm doing!"

In Janet's case, her break with work allowed a fixing-up so that she could return to the job she loved. In other instances, a break to re-energize seems to be required first, for mental health and second for exploration. George G. felt he was on the brink of collapse when he left his company. Ronda S. took a one-year sabbatical to regain her sense of control.

●●●

*Sean F., professional photographer.*

Having worked as a freelance photographer and photojournalist, Sean returned to school to study video productions. "I got hired by ABC and traveled the world as a cameraman for hard news. I saw the seamy, violent side of life; people killed for no reason. When I came back from these assignments, I resigned voluntarily. I didn't want to pick up a camera again. I took a year off, not to figure out what to do with my life, but to regain my health. My value system underwent an entire re-analysis."

While few of us will ever be in Sean's position, the point is made here that sometimes our first action step might be a decision in which we feel compelled to remove ourselves ... but that's the only decision we make. The direction remains uncertain.

●●●

*Gary R., former executive in the recording industry.*

Although admittedly miserable in his work for some time, Gary's first action to take control of the situation finally came during an annual international meeting in Greece, which he organized for the company.

"I was very uptight and uneasy during the convention. There was unnecessary pressure created from top management. You could feel the anxiety. It was created, excuse the term, by nothing more than corporate bullshit. The day after the convention broke, we had a meeting to discuss the next year's strategy. From experience, I knew that everything we said there and all the volumes of notes would never take place. What bullshit! It was an exercise in futility."

"I remember leaving that room and feeling that way. Outwardly, everyone patting each other on the back, but it was all phony."

He went to his hotel room, put on his running clothes, and told his wife not to ask any questions. "I told her I was going out and when I came back—no matter how long it took—things would be different."

Around the city of Athens he ran. Faster. Harder. Longer. "Between the meeting, the nonsense, and the running, I knew I didn't need it any more. I didn't like the politics. I felt above what was happening. I was watching them playing a game and I didn't want to be one of the players. Everybody had this deck of cards and they were dishing them out. But no matter how often they were shuffled, you always got the same hand. I didn't want to play anymore."

When he returned to the States, Gary knew he was leaving. "I didn't know the exact date, I didn't know what I was going to do, but I knew I was leaving. Fellow employees would see me grinning and they'd ask, 'What's with you, happy face?' I'd tell them, 'I'm in a new place. Just accept it. I'm in a new place.'"

## Stage Three: Begin Active Exploration

Regardless of what first step you take to regain some sense of control—whether saying "no" to another assignment or asking for a sabbatical—exploration of potential actions is now required.

This chapter contains possible exploration methods which others have found helpful in creating changes within their work or job. But remember, work is only part of the picture. In the next chapter, we'll examine "living" and the balance of both.

Dependent upon the depth of the "pit" and the possible causes, the exploration process will vary in both complexity and length of time. However, all exploration must include both external measures as well as internal dialogue. Your happiness and sense of living is a reality you first create from the inside.

# Talk About Your Feelings and Possible Solutions

This is not a call for en masse gripe sessions or circular conversations that only reinforce how miserable you are. Instead, the object behind this step is to get a different perspective by receiving feedback and fresh insight from someone outside your situation. It also allows you to verbally "try out" possible actions and see how you feel about them.

•••

*Samantha "Sam" E. (fictitious name), loan officer, suburban bank.*

Sam joined the bank just as the local area was being "discovered" by residents of a neighboring city. Within short order, the bank's real-estate loan portfolio grew as new homes attracted newcomers to the town. Sam's manager realized that it was impossible for the department to keep up with the processing of documents and added another clerk.

Within a year, the help was still not enough. Pressure from clients mounted daily. Deadlines were critical. Sam worked overtime almost every night and still took paperwork home with her. The manager insisted that money was not available for additional help. More and more, Sam found herself dreading each day, forcing herself into the office, having no time for friends, and requiring more sleep than normal.

"I didn't mind pressure. I've always worked hard. But at least at the end of the day it was over. But now, I'm tired down to my bones."

As a first action, she talked herself into leaving work on her desk and spent a weekend at her mountain cabin. When she returned to town, Sam contacted a former associate and friend who understood the banking business.

"I shared how I felt and he gave me feedback which I hadn't considered before. By talking about my feelings I realized that I didn't want to leave my job but that I was tremendously out of control. He provided me with some thoughts on how I might approach my boss and also validated my tentative decision not to work overtime anymore. I think I needed to hear that so I could, in fact, give myself permission to slow down. My soul is worth more than making additional money for the bank."

She also met with a stress consultant to understand just how she could change some of her work habits. "I had added to my dilemma because I didn't speak out when things became too much for me to handle."

Because Sam basically liked her chosen work, this exploration step required primarily the presence of a wisely chosen listener selected for his/her ability to provide honest, unbiased feedback. But for the deeper pits, the more severe symptoms, exploration might require professional help.

## Seek Help With Work/Job Decisions – and Read

In exploring potential changes that will promote integration in our lives and a sense of control in our work/job, there are two areas that might require some outside professional assistance. The most obvious one is in the assessment of our talents, abilities, and possible career choices.

The growing interest in career management has produced numerous excellent books and countless consulting firms which many people have found helpful, if not essential, to the process of finding their true "work." Herein lies my dilemma: How do I explore this step with you in the most meaningful way?

I, too, turned to others for assistance.

One might also consider a career-management firm. But first, the following guidelines might be helpful:

- A contract that states exactly what you will be getting for your money.

- A program that enables you to take control of the job search process and use it many times during your life.

- A logically structured and sequenced program that is broken down into do-able steps which build on each other.

- A complete program that addresses the issue of career choice as well as sound job-hunting techniques.

- A flexible, personalized program that addresses your individual needs.

- Qualified counselors who understand adult development and the career management process.

## When And/Or Why Might Someone Consider Such Professional Help In The Exploration Process?

Oftentimes, exploring on your own is a problem in that you get lost, rejected, or stuck. Working through a process together keeps you rolling and doing something. It's also the old forest-for-the-trees dilemma. A good career-management firm helps the client look at issues in the environment, but most of all, at skills. There is no such thing as job security, only skill. And one can learn the skill of exploration. After all, there is also no such thing as the permanent job. The process will be needed again.

## What Advice Can You Give To Help The Exploration Process?

The exploration process does not necessarily mean you will change direction. Rather, the process could very well help you articulate what you need in the present situation.

According to one career consultant: "Being able to say what you want is highly important. For example, a re-entry woman in industrial sales had three things that contributed to her 'pit': a poor boss; no opportunity to interact with others; and a car for an office. We had her attend meetings with other salespeople, where she found that her job was better than most for that line of work. We coached her so that she could talk with her boss in a non-defensive manner. She then joined professional groups and organized her time and her car better so that her environment improved."

It is equally important to maintain momentum during exploration. Keep talking, keep working, but always doing something. Inertia is everyone's greatest enemy in a process like this. Write one letter, make one phone call, attend one class, but move. Otherwise, you'll start a downward spiral.

Finally, be thinking about these variables in the exploration process: the work environment, roles, skills, values, and interest issues. Under work environment, consider what physical surroundings, what size organization, and what emotional tones are important to you. Do you prefer to work with people, ideas, or things? In considering your role, ask yourself in what way do you wish to interact with others: as a manager, a resource of information, a promoter, etc.

When it comes to skills which can be transferred from one job to another, look at more than just measurable, technical ability. There are personal skills (stick-to-itness, analytical or creative ability, honesty, etc.) as well as skills in planning, writing, organizing, speaking, and others. Remember, the skills that come naturally, easily, and are most enjoyable are the ones you really prefer. The more those preferred skills are utilized, the more energized and challenged you will be.

Lastly, look at interest issues—those bigger-than-myself causes that capture your emotions and passions, such as the environment, abused children, human rights, hunger. Like preferred skills, if there are such interest issues in your life, you will be more energized if your work deals with these issues.

## Seek Help With Life Context

The second area which might require a new look and professional assistance is self-discovery. The understanding of who we are in relation to everything else can very well make a difference in the work and balance choices we make as well as our attitude toward those choices.

To explain, I'd like you to think about a snowflake. We know that each snowflake is different. In fact, let's assume that there will never be another snowflake like the one that is right now drifting to earth.

As the snowflake dances on the winter air, it behaves just like a snowflake should, bowing and dipping in turn with its other snowflakes. Once upon the ground, the snowflake becomes part of a snowdrift. As the wind whistles and the temperature drops, the flakes press tighter against each other.

Our snowflake keeps its identity, but the context in which it must now operate is different. Not only is it no longer alone, but there is a different response needed to the current situation. In the winter's dance, Little Snowflake could spin lightly around, showing off whatever dancing talent it had. Now, its talents are called upon to bear the weight of other snowflakes, to respond in a different fashion.

The analogy could continue with the snowflake changing into a drop of water that sits in a mud puddle, is evaporated and becomes a cloud, later returning to earth as rain. In all these instances, the context changes under which Little Snowflake lives, and moves, and has its being.

The same concept applies to humans. By looking at the movement of our life and the context in which we interact with others, we begin to realize the continuity and purpose and meaning which we bring to each day.

Perhaps this concept is easier to understand if I share Robert Wendorf's insight. After all, it is based upon his personal experience with life context that Robert discontinued his Beverly Hills practice and moved to a slower-paced city, where he could concentrate on these issues with clients.

●●●

*Robert W., psychotherapist.*

"My journey through 'the pits' wasn't confined to any one time. It was rather a period of experiencing some things that were very foreign to me. I began exploring yoga with a teacher from India.... meeting people who were putting higher and higher priorities on their health, worship, exercise, and things that I had always considered secondary."

"A shift was taking place in who I was. It was agony and ecstasy. Painful. Exciting. Frightening. Questioning. There was no single turning point but rather a series. One turning point was seeing that I had the practice I had long since sought, that I was making good money, that I could play the game, that I had invested a lot of money in personal therapy, and still something was missing."

He added a side note that clinicians either confront their own anxieties with therapy, leave the field or move into administration.

"What I was discovering was that I was truly a part of the process of life. That life is expressing itself through me. This was something new to me."

"When I was counseled by other professionals, no one dealt with a change in context. No one ever said 'who are you?' It is necessary to know that I am part of a bigger picture, that I go through periods of doubt and confusion, but that nevertheless, life is unfolding in me. I have value! This was what was missing for me. You must hear it over and over again before it becomes integrated."

"This is what I do in my psychotherapy and transition counseling. I assist people in understanding and experiencing themselves as a unique part of the overall process of life."

●●●

Robert is not a lone voice crying from a mountain top. Now there are counselors and therapists who guide individuals in understanding the movement of their lives.

Other avenues of life-context exploration are available through workshops designed by people like Robert.

There is value in all of them, even if deciding which to attend is difficult. Since we respond differently to certain formats, personalities, and methods of presentation, it might take several attempts before you find a workshop that strikes a personal chord. But it is well worth the effort.

Journaling is a personal method that has worked for me ever since I went to an Intensive Journal Workshop presented by Dialogue House. The Intensive Journal program has been taught to thousands of participants around the world, in colleges, branches of the armed forces, hospitals, prisons, and churches. The Intensive Journal process provides a systematic yet individualized and private approach for clarifying where you are now in your life, determining what resources are present, and deciding on new directions. No, you don't have to be a writer to use it and no, you don't write in it every day. But as the need arises, I have found myself perched on my bed or sitting on the beach with my journal in hand, watching feelings and connections flow—without judgment or censorship—from my pen. Amazing what I discover! But remember, this method is what I have decided works for me. Your choices are, and must be, uniquely patterned to you. And when you see the patterns, you can make your work WORK for you.

Certainly help of this nature might not take priority among the action steps required for your immediate situation, but my heart (as well as my research) insists that I include this step. To paraphrase Socrates: "The unexamined life is a life not worth living."

## Take Exploratory Courses

A corresponding reason for the depression and helplessness is that options appear limited. A way to alter that perception is by examining other fields of interest which have been ignored or forgotten. There is tremendous power in knowledge.

In trying to work her way through the "pit" as director of communication, Cheryl P. enrolled in a fiction class. Her limited on-the-job writing was then expanded by this extracurricular activity. To her surprise, she discovered that she relished each course assignment and the desire to write became even stronger.

By the end of the first day in a course entitled, "Career Transitions for Educators," Ronda S. decided to request a leave of absence. "In the workshop, I started to believe I had other strengths. Maybe I did have other things that I could do!"

Charles D. learned the same thing. Even before leaving his $6-million corporation, he had started taking night classes in psychology. "After I quit, I went to Europe for my first vacation in ten years. I came home with the realization that I didn't want to be a marketing executive. The psychology course had touched an old but never-satisfied interest. I entered college as a full-time student to earn a M.A. in counseling."

Not all exploratory classes open doors.

Loan Officer Samantha, in trying to evaluate potential solutions for her out-of-balance situation, decided to take a course in surveying. "I had a real-estate background before coming to the bank and I was getting more involved in that field with the type of loan documents I was handling. Since I also liked being outdoors, the thought of land surveying seemed appealing."

She took the course and found the practical work to be dull and uninteresting. "But I felt better. It was just as important to look at that area and then decide I didn't want it."

## Practice Networking

With or without professional help, the results of the exploration process can explode tenfold by utilizing networking. A network is an information web, the process of equalizing opportunity by sharing knowledge. One reaches out to others, researches and learns through the sharing of experiences, broadens contacts, and gains a wider view of the world than before.

•••

*Charles D., now counselor and video producer.*

"I knew the home-improvement industry inside and out when I left. But I had blinders on to the rest of the world. I didn't know much about such things as consultants, colleges, and cable-video programs. So I made a decision to grow."

He cut his ties with the industry and instead made a goal to meet two new interesting people a week. "Authors, athletes, someone written up in the paper, whoever intrigues me ...I called and asked them to lunch. Without knowing it, I began creating a network."

•••

*Ronda S., now a sales representative for an education-equipment company.*

Networking became a way of life for Ronda when she took her leave of absence and moved to the same city as her boyfriend. Prior to leaving the school, she sent a note to her friends and colleagues, asking for the names and addresses of anyone they knew in her new town who might be a general connection.

"Armed with that list, I contacted these somewhat-new 'friends.' At first, my concept in meeting people had been you-are-what-you-work. Since I no longer had work, with these folks I practiced getting out and saying what my skills were. Not only was I practicing getting out there and informally investigating, but I was learning to convince others that I could do something besides teach."

She also began collecting information through corporate interview—not asking for a job, but merely seeking information about specific industries. Additionally, by attending the meetings of a wide variety of professional associations which encouraged guests, she was able to expand her circle of acquaintances and her potential work ideas.

"I also spoke with educators who had made a transition, asking them what had been most successful for them. Some even let me sit in on their job and observe if I thought I might be interested in that occupation."

"I'd even go talk with employment agencies, if for no other reason than to practice talking about my skills. That way, I became even clearer in my own mind what my potential really was."

Simple informational networking also empowers by expanding personal horizons. In a conversation with Jennifer, a successful bank manager, I discovered she'd been an art major who entered banking because a divorce settlement forced her to support a family. "So I guess I'll just have to stay here," she sighed. "I don't know anything else to do."

She was subsequently astonished to consider that there might be ways to blend her love of art with her financial background: as an art appraiser and consultant; a consultant on corporate art collections; a buyer for galleries; etc.

"Why, I never thought of such things," she exclaimed. She also had never considered looking beyond the obvious. Informational networking might have opened new vistas.

## Surround Yourself With Positive People

The exploration process is difficult enough without negative feedback from the outside. As Mark Twain so aptly insisted, "Keep away from people who belittle your ambitions. Small people try to do that, but really great people make you feel that you, too, can become great."

The search for the work of our lives and attendant balance requires us to travel through peaks and valleys. Develop a support network of individuals who will encourage you, who might even be going through the same process so that you no longer feel alone. One career-counseling firm feels so strongly about this that they gather their clients together at a weekly informal party for the sole purpose of sharing ups and downs.

## Use Both Sides of Your Brain

There's a tendency to reduce our exploration to the logical, head-felt actions. Period. But we are also people of emotions, creativity (no matter how stifled) and feelings. In fact, no matter how analytical you might be in the present out-of-balance "pit," the rock-bottom reality is that you do not feel happy. Period.

To get in touch with those feelings, as well as to affirm your own growth process, try success imaging. Cut out magazine pictures of people who show how you'd like to feel, what you'd like to be doing. At night, think of yourself in a place of balance, control and energy. Feel what it is like to be there. In fact, as you explore alternative changes in direction, feel (not think about) how it would be if such a change were to occur.

From personal experience, I know that more than one choice has been altered because it just didn't feel right. We have a lot more power in both hemispheres of our brain than we give credit to.

# Reward Yourself Each Time You Stretch

Why is it that we think of rewarding children when they have performed in an exceptional manner (for their specific ability) but forget to reward ourselves for doing something that requires extra efforts? That's what stretching is—doing something which we find hard to do. It might be writing a letter, talking to a counselor, reading an article, discussing how we feel, even pushing to get to an exercise class because, instinctively, you know your body needs to be renewed.

Whatever it is, Ronda S. shares a way of accounting and rewarding these stretches. "To influence my behavior, I pick out something that I know should do but don't. Then, each time I do it, I put a sticker on the calendar. Four stickers and I acknowledge myself: getting my nails done; going to the theater; anything that rewards my effort."

# Be Patient and Flexible

The decision-making process does not happen overnight. There are many avenues to explore, tentative action steps to consider. A choice is a process, not an end result. As you learn more about yourself, the choices will change. Rigid decisions are like icicles—brittle, stiff, cold and subject to shattering or melting. A flexible posture within this process, however, allows you to unfold like a sailboat spinnaker to capture all the wind. However, flexible does not mean that you never make a choice; that you vacillate like a will-o'-wisp and therefore never move forward.

In summary, at this point in the process, you have made no decisions other than to analyze, re-energize, take whatever immediate step is called for to gain some small measure of control, and to explore. There are still other parts of you—the other components that make up living—that need to be considered.

# Summary

1. Stage One: Analysis of the situation. Accept responsibility for your role in the pit:

    - Look at attitudes.

    - Look at your response to personal history.

    - Look at your response to social pressure.

    - Determine the level of expectation.

    - Determine if the "pit" is really work/job or a cover-up.

    - Take action to re-energize.

2. Stage Two: Determine the first action and do it.

    - If possible, start with your workplace. Throwing the baby out with the bath water is not a great idea if you can change the bathtub or adjust the water temperature.

3. Stage Three: Begin active exploration

    - Talk about your feelings and possible solutions.

    - Seek help with work/job decisions and analysis.

    - Seek help in understanding life context.

    - Take exploratory courses.

    - Practice networking.

    - Surround yourself with positive people.

    - Use both sides of your brain.

    - Reward yourself for stretching.

    - Be patient and flexible.

# Chapter Six
# This Thing Called "Live"

---

*The truth is that life is delicious, horrible, charming, frightful,*
*sweet, bitter, and that it is everything.*

– Anatole France

---

What would you say if I asked you, "tell me what it means to be fully alive?"
Years ago, I had the wonderful opportunity to teach a session under the approval
of author John Powell, S.J., In the Fully Alive Experience, I asked this very question
of participants. I divided them into groups, handed them a sheet of newsprint,
and said, "go to it."

Within fifteen minutes, after much laughter, the results were posted around the
room: eating all the ice cream you want; going to the theater; backpacking;
hugging the family; driving with the top down; telling jokes; solving problems;
loving without expecting; bubble baths; experiencing the full range of feelings;
and on and on.

Of the twenty-eight people present, no one said anything about working.

Why is it that we think working and living are mutually exclusive?

Counterpoint: If I had asked the participants what does success mean. I'd be
willing to bet that the majority of the responses would not include any of the
"fully alive" activities.

To be fair to the wonderful people gathered on that spring Saturday morning, I
think the group might have eventually come up with some correlation. But not
at first. We are conditioned to think of success first in terms of achievement,
fame and fortune.

Notice these three words: achievement, fame, fortune. They are words of quantity, of more and most; recognizable symbols to the outside world. But they may not mean quality.

The truth is that there is as much "success" in catching a trout, comforting a friend, or kneeling before whatever Higher Power you profess, as there is in making a killing on Wall Street, heading up a corporation, or closing a crucial sale.

The truth is that there can be just as much "aliveness" in designing a car, teaching a class, or developing a marketing campaign as there is in skinny-dipping, lobster dinners, and naps in a hammock.

What throws us askew and out of the hammock, into an either-or-posture, is a continual lack of integration. And we get that way by the choices we make—with our work/job choice as the cornerstone.

Case in point: I had been invited to attend a meeting with a gentleman who, according to his definition and those around him, was a "success" because he was paid some well-above average fee for his speeches and seminars. "Okay," I thought. "Sounds fine so far."

Throughout the dinner, he told me how he plotted marketing strategy, how many phone calls he made a day, how he spent weekends (he's not married) making contacts for business development. "I'll be one of the most successful, high paid speakers on the circuit."

A very talented musician closed the evening. His final number, which brought down the house, as well as tears to many eyes, was a song he had written about his friend, a handicapped child. "Wow," I said, wiping my eyes. "What did you think of that song?" The middle-aged gentleman turned to me with a puzzled look.

"Oh, I didn't pay any attention to that. I was making notes about some of his stage techniques which I might use."

His response saddened me. Single-minded attention to being a success had lost him a powerful, magical experience.

Don't get me wrong. Ambition, a desire to be recognized for our efforts, and hard work are all admirable qualities. But it's the over-concentration for extended periods of time that distorts the picture, disconnects us, creates the unhappy dichotomy.

A colleague observed to me: "Businessmen and women today are the world's greatest jugglers. They juggle enormous job responsibilities, financial demands, community involvement, spousal needs, parenting chores, social commitments, and more. It often seems that they are being pulled apart—that everybody is taking a piece of them—until there is nothing left for themselves."

More and more it is becoming clear that for the executive and professional, there is really no definite separation between one's personal and business life. They are tremendously and significantly interwoven. It is just as important to manage the business of your life as it is to manage the life of your business.

In considering your current work/job life, what can you add, alter, or amend to give you more control and happiness? Is there any way you can structure your work/job so as to add some of these important areas into it?

This latter question bears careful consideration. First, consider these following scenarios:

1. It's a beautiful, clear, blue, and white Colorado winter day. The skiers are whisking down slopes of new powder. Two skiers slip into the lift-line and are carried upward for another run.

2. Night falls on a wave-battered Northern California coast. A man and a woman walk out to a rock outcropping overlooking the ocean as the sun sinks below the horizon.

3. Two volleyball teams spike, dive, and sweat on a sand court. Spectators, siding with neither team, applaud the effort as well as the results. The players are female/male, young/old, black/white, excited.

Do any of these scenarios sound like work? Dr. Tom Isgar, a management consultant from Florida, planned it that way. And he got paid in the bargain. "We can make our work more like the not-work experiences we strive for. We can redesign some of our work so that it is fun."

And just what was Dr. Isgar doing?

In the first example, he was discussing career/life planning with a senior executive as well as the performance of several subordinates.

In the second, this scene was part of a four-hour drive down California's scenic coast highway during which time they conducted the initial program planning which led to a three-year organization improvement plan.

And in the last scene, the volleyball game was part of a team-building exercise within a large organization.

He depends on personal criteria to make work fun and healthier. "I like to play tennis so I design workshops with tennis time. I like fresh fruit so I ask that we have fruit and juice. Without exception I have experienced a positive response from clients. By acting on the items which make work more fun for me, I suggest ways in which others can make their own work fun. Most importantly, in doing so I improve the quality of my own working life while working with clients to improve the quality of theirs."

## So Where Does It All Lead?

Only by considering our total self at the same time we seek either the "work" of our life or a "job" can we hope to be free to live. Sure, there will be times when we are tremendously out of balance, but the trick is to recognize just what part of our life has been given too much power or has been ignored.

"But wait," you might say. "There's just too much to consider. I can't get a handle on the big picture of my life."

Got it. So, here are questions to stimulate much awareness as to the "now" of our lives. I keep a journal and answer these questions twice a year. It also then helps me to realize just where I am spending my time and what are my priorities. I also have a simple monthly log in which I take the areas of my life and collect just what happened. It has a wonderful way of allowing me to realize that time does not just pass me by. Often, I am amazed at how much I am in control and how integrated I actually am!

Reflective questions (for year-end or mid-year check)

1. What were your top priorities in time, money and energy?

2. What were your finest accomplishments?

3. What were your biggest surprises?

4. What were your biggest disappointments?

5. What were your most significant decisions?

6. What people were you closest to?

7. What stressed you the most?

8. Where did you travel for fun?

9. What lessons have you learned?

10. Who or what were you most angry at?

11. What did you procrastinate on?

12. Summarize the year (or six-month period) in a word.

---

*"It's not enough to be busy. So are the ants.*

*What are you busy about?"*

*— Thoreau*

---

## Summary

1. Working and quality living can go together but out doesn't happen by chance.

2. Integrating our work and life also implies knowing when we are out of control and which areas of our life have been neglected.

3. Work and life integration is not a static condition. Like a sailboat that requires constant handling, we need to constantly take our pulse and check in with our head AND heart.

# Chapter Seven
# Eeney, Meeney, Miney, Mo

*We are but the instruments of heaven;*
*our work is not design but destiny.*

— *Bulwer-Lytton, English poet*

I doubt anyone would ever accuse my husband of being a clothes horse. When we first met, his wardrobe was tasteful but sparse. In short order, my love of bargains and gift-giving soon began to fill his closet. "Look," he said one morning in frustration, "I love you, but please don't buy me any more shirts. How I hate to get up and make a decision!"

I hadn't thought about it that way. The opportunity to choose can be too much.

Although I like Bulwer-Lytton's quote because it capsulizes my idea of "giftedness," I nevertheless wish heaven could be more specific. Sometimes it doesn't seem fair that Biblical Samuel got a call in the middle of the night and bingo! His career was signed, sealed, and delivered. For many of us, locating the work of our lives is a trial-and-error process. There are just so many choices.

And so we unwrap our giftedness slowly, unfolding tissue, peering between each layer, waiting to catch our breath before we see the actual gift. Some move on and find other gifts to open. It's not unusual.

A recent article published in The Executive Female reported that ten successful professionals (male and female) all responded "no" when asked, "Is what you are doing now what you originally had expected to be doing?" Some career counselors estimate that as many as seven major switches occur in a lifetime.

For others, giftedness is a present which can be immediately unwrapped and used with enthusiasm. It comes from a Greek word, "Enthusiasms," meaning "possessed by a god within." (See heaven did have a say-so after all.) We can indeed be possessed enthused—by our work.

Sandy, a single parent raising three teenagers, has taught elementary school for over twenty years. Ask her about her work and her face glows. "Why, I love it. It's my life." She's bewildered that I even had to ask! Lyricist Sammy Kahn once told an audience that "if they saw how much fun I have writing songs, I think they wouldn't pay me." From the time my gynecologist followed his grandfather around on house calls, he knew he wanted to be a doctor. Hundreds of babies later, my doctor friend can still say eagerly, "I love it! Women are wonderful!"

Lest you think this "possessed" group has it easy in the decision-making department, don't forget that they, too, are also responsible for maintaining balance by the choices made in other life areas.

## So What Now?

Hopefully by now you're beginning to become aware of what might be the causes for your pit or where you've let a critical piece of your life slip by you.

This chapter provides an overview for making decisions within two settings: the corporate (where you work for someone) and the entrepreneurial (where you work for yourself). We'll also look at some examples of "unfolding" so that you might observe the trial-and-error process.

If experience is the best teacher, then I've assembled some good tutors for you. Pay attention to how they explored, what choices were made for balance, what imbalance might still remain. Most of all, consider this your support team. You're not alone.

But first, let's add two more possibilities into the cerebral processor—to prepare you for this unfolding.

## More In The Exploration Process
## Creativity

In the last chapter, how did you feel when you read about Dr. Isgar's ability to add personal pleasure to his work routine? Did you wish that you could put some fun into your current or prospective work? Did you notice that he structured work activities to include recreation and nutrition? These are parts of the physical area which often become ignored with rapid-paced work. Or perhaps you might have thought, "Oh, that's easy for him. He's a consultant."

May I suggest that what allowed Isgar to even consider such additions was not his actual profession. Burned-out, stressed-out, in-the-pits consultants exist everywhere. No, the consulting practice was not the root for such work decisions. It was his ability to think creatively.

The creative person sees beyond the obvious, finds connections, think in terms of possibilities rather than impossibilities. The person who can channel a right-brain activity says "why not" instead of "cannot!".

Consider these creative choices: A psychologist takes his clients mountain climbing. He loves the outdoors and they learn to trust, communicate, and risk. A sales executive is an amateur photographer. With permission from her clients, she takes candid as well as artistic shots within client companies. She sends them the photos as gifts and she makes a lot of sales. Jane needs exercise, but the class times at the local recreation center conflict with work and family. She talks to the personnel department and gets approval to lead an aerobics class twice a week at lunch time for interested colleagues.

Can you see the integration of other life areas? All connections. All creative wanderings that put many pieces of quality life into a work setting.

Think creatively about potential new work. Think connections. Colonel Sanders decided that other people would enjoy his mom's fried chicken. A wine press at a harvest festival became Gutenberg's inspiration for the printing press. An ex-surfer runs a wind surfing school in Hawaii.

But creativity also requires a willingness to depart from the normal course of action and remain courageous in the face of criticism, skepticism, and doubting Thomases. You can recognize the doubters by the words they use.

Killer phrases are everywhere:

- That's stupid.

- It will never work.

- We don't have the time.

- We tried it before.

- It'll cost too much money.

Care to add some killer phrases which you've heard recently? This exercise will alert you to the words others use to point out shortcomings rather than benefits; why some things won't work rather than how to make things better. Come on, think of two:

1. _____

2. _____

Just as there are trigger-happy doubters on the outside, there is a real sharp-shooter on the inside. More frequently than not, an idea is squashed by mental thumbs-down inside of us. When you begin to think beyond the obvious, particularly about choices that will change your "work" or life, have you said this to yourself:

- People will think I'm crazy.

- Who do I think I am to try that!

- My wife (husband) will kill me.

- My parents (lover, mentor, whoever) will be terribly disappointed in me.

- As soon as I bring up my idea, someone will kick it apart.

- What if it doesn't work!?

Now it's your turn. Care to venture any killer phrases which you use to halt further consideration of a new or different direction? Go ahead, try for two:

1. _____

2. _____

If you can recognize killer phrases, perhaps you can halt the guerrilla warfare which prevents you from at least exploring creative choices.

# The Road Not Taken

Two concepts rest in this phrase. We owe the first to Robert Frost, the crusty New England poet who penned that taking the road less traveled had "made all the difference." Breaking with tradition, following a creative path, going against the tide, doing the unexpected are all less-traveled roads—roads not ordinarily taken by the majority. It might be that your choices entail leaving the well-worn career path or lifestyle and striking out in a new direction.

The second concept cares nothing about how many people travel down a road. Rather, it invites you to reexamine a path not taken in the past and to consider walking down it now! This concept is seldom discussed and yet holds tremendous potential in understanding the movement of our lives and in making choices.

The movement of your life, up to this very minute, has been marked by decisions, some made by you, some made by others, and some made totally by circumstance. These decisions sent you down certain paths—paths which led to where you are today. However, this does not mean that you cannot go back and explore the road you didn't take! The conditions which created the road taken long ago might indeed have altered or even vanished.

For example, in looking back over stages of my life, I suddenly remembered that my father had wanted me to take singing lessons and I had refused. Painfully shy, I died at piano recitals. The thought of having to perform in another one was too much. But I feel different now about myself.

To walk down that "road not taken," I took a singing lesson. I took lots of them. Great fun. Now—where possible, I incorporate music in my programs.

At face value this might seem like a rather mundane road to explore. But I have always felt a twinge of envy at Broadway stars and cabaret singers. No more. No so-called vain regrets. Dealing with that buried memory was as important as if I had discovered a new talent and direction.

What a win-win proposition! Here's one other consideration in the "road not taken" concept: nothing is forever. Just because I decided that at this time in my life singing is not a profession for me, there's wonderful freedom in knowing that I can go back at any time and once again, try journeying down that road.

# The Corporate Career – Moving Around Inside

## Any Which Way You Want

One of the more common and dangerous errors in seeking the "work" of your life or giftedness is to think that there are only two alternatives when you work for someone else: out or up. The "out" choice to another organization might still not tap your skills if they remain unidentified or if you're holding onto damaging attitudes. "Out" to entrepreneurship might mean longer hours, less freedom, greater financial risk. As for "up," long considered the only legitimate way to success, hear this: it's not the only way.

Let's try that again: up is not the only way. And who would know this better than Dr. Beverly Kaye, author of a book by the very title and a nationally recognized corporate career-management consultant. For over four plus decades, Dr. Kaye has worked with hundreds of corporations across the United States to help employees discover their preferred skills and point those talents in the direction indicated by the individual's entire "life" picture. That direction might be any which way BUT up! Her newest work, found in two books: *Love'Em. Don't Lose'Em; Love It. Don't Leave It*, builds on her fascination with engagement and retention.

"Society does people a real injustice by telling them that the vertical, traditional move is the only way. After all, just how many people can fit on the point of a pyramid? We can't all move up—but we can all grow. There should always be a challenge in your career, something that requires your all. But it doesn't have to come from the next rung on the ladder above you."

In addition to the standard vertical move into a higher salary and title, Dr. Kaye lists five other directions to consider: moving across (lateral); growing in place (enrichment); looking around (exploratory); moving down (realignment); and lastly, moving out (relocation).

## The Lateral Move

"A sideways move more often makes more sense than people realize," says Kaye. "It allows you to develop new skills, broaden your base of knowledge, change geographical locations and/or colleagues, and maybe even reach a faster growth area of the company. For example, a loan office might move to another branch. He's still a loan officer, but the branch, customers, and employees are different."

In other cases, a lateral move can take existing skills and transfer them into a different position but with equivalent pay and status. Debbie G. (fictitious name) was a marketing officer who gambled on a possible decrease in pay to transfer to the personnel relations office so that she might work more with people. Not only did she maintain her present salary, but her newfound enthusiasm for the personally rewarding position led to a dramatic rise in salary and grade level in less than a year.

Kaye insists: "Sudden benefits are not surprising when people are doing what they really like and do well. Organizations only benefit when their employees are in the 'like' and 'do-well' jobs."

## The Enrichment Move

Instead of moving across, enhancing the current position could be a strong option. You already observed a number of cases where individuals added portions of other life areas to their "work." Kaye believes that there are also ways to make a current job more exciting, more challenging. "But the individual has to devise these; the company isn't going to do it for him or her," she says.

Karen W., a communications specialist for an international manufacturer of computer products, decided that just writing the company newsletter was not enough challenge. "I accepted responsibility for the corporate identity package which would give me a lot of visibility within the company. I also volunteered to take on a brochure for the personnel department. Now, my paycheck is almost like a bonus. I truly enjoy what I'm doing."

As we noted earlier, the enrichment of your job might mean adding things other than what might normally be entitled as "work." A priest in an inner-city parish began to experience the pangs of burnout. So much to do, so little to do it with, so hard to reach the people who needed help. To correct that imbalance, he began getting back into a pastime long since neglected – music. Weekend jam sessions with some of the neighbors attracted a crowd. Within short order, he bartered an old piano from a local bar, placed it in the parish hall and began offering piano lessons to children in the area. By enhancing his current position with the use of another talent, his flock is increasing and so is his level of satisfaction.

# The Exploration Move

In the exploration option, an employee researches new opportunities to use already uncovered talents as well as to discover hidden or dormant skills. With Dr. Kaye's help, an unhappy computer draftsman finally realized that his skills were totally people-oriented. A move to the planning department dramatically changed the work field, and yet his satisfaction was still not hitting number ten on the charts. Another workshop refined those "people skills" as "teaching skills." He then opted to put on mini-seminars introducing new employees to the department. In this case, both the exploration and enrichment option made sense.

# The Realignment Move

Ever so slowly, our changing value system is making it more feasible to look at downscaling as a way for gaining control and balance within one's life. Although the move is still difficult because it's the exact opposite of the cultural programming, "downshifting" is catching hold.

"It's hard for the failure stigma not to be attached to a downward move," relates Dr. Kaye. "But both employers and individuals can benefit from taking a healthier view of this move. A higher position does not always bring the anticipated personal rewards. There are those who find out after a promotion to a managerial slot that they really don't like it at all. They don't like the pressure, the time demands, the intrusions on their personal life."

The former president of a large publishing company explained his choice for a downward move in these terms. "My ego wasn't satisfied by titles. While I was president, the company became more successful. We rose from $8 million to $40 million. And I hated it. I became all consumed by the bottom line. At my request, I moved into a division with ten people."

●●●

*Another composite example:*

A medical researcher, noted for his brilliance in new-product development, made the inevitable move through the ranks until reaching a position where he managed an entire research division working on cardiovascular instrumentation. A different type of paperwork poured across his desk. Employee performance needed to be monitored. Orders had to be given, work teams harmonized, and salary reviews made. A classic pit was in the making: stress; fatigue; irritability; strained family relationships; and much imbalance.

Let the truth be known: he wanted to be a researcher, not a manager. Thankfully, he realigned himself back into the old spot. To his astonishment, his wife broke open the champagne. The researcher had felt that she wanted him to make the top slot when in reality, she secretly wanted him back where he was happy but was afraid he didn't want to move down.

## The Relocation Move

If the company had not been progressive enough to restructure job categories to accommodate people like the medical researcher, his move might have been out.

Such was the case of a director of engineering in a large computer firm. He loved tinkering with the product as a hands-on designer. His interpersonal skills were strong one-on-one, but as a manager he swam like a landed salmon. His outward move put him back in the water as vice president of a small computer company, where he is integrally involved in the design and marketing of the product.

Dr. Kaye admits it's not easy convincing a company that a move out of the corporation has as much validity as the other options. "They worry that they'll lose their best, most valuable employees. But if a person is unhappy, the organization isn't going to get a full effort from him/her anyway. And sometimes, the only position a person can take is a path out of the company."

●●●

*Mike B., now senior industrial-relations executive for a consulting firm.*

When we first met Mike, he had determined that his first responsibility for getting out of the "people" pit was to rearrange his reaction to the vice president's autocratic style and temper tantrums.

As a newcomer in the area, he began a concerted effort to attend whatever evening meetings he could find within his profession, started to network on weekends, and also explored lateral moves within the corporation.

The corporate search turned up a dismal picture. It appeared that autocracy plus a rigid caste system dominated the corporate culture. Long-time employees, plus a friend in the personnel department, warned him not to "make waves." "Just accept the good salary and keep your mouth shut."

For a talented person with strong ambition, that option was tasteless. Instead, he determined to remain until such time as a highly attractive growth opportunity presented itself. In the meantime, he accepted assignments which others didn't want and kept the corporate game in play.

"When I finally resigned to accept a challenging position that had been offered through networking, my work spoke for itself. I left well, despite the conflicts with my vice president."

Whether the move is up, down, around, across, or out, we do have choices and the responsibility to ASK for what we want. Granted, we might have to seek outside assistance in determining just what we really want to ask for and the reality of that request. (The self-administered Career Leverage Inventory developed by Kaye is just one example of many available external resources used by career counselors.)

In whatever fashion, by whatever means you move toward a decision, the point remains. "There are multiple ways, endless paths to follow. It makes very little sense in today's business world to limit yourself to an upward path," Kaye concludes.

## The Corporate Career – Moving in From The Outside

## The Financial Move

George G. returned to his uncle's corporation because his public-relations practice fell short of its mark. Sandy R. opted for a sales position with a manufacturing company when the income from teaching proved too miniscule for a single homeowner. Ronda S., a speech therapist, felt the same financial crunch as well as a host of other imbalances.

Although financial need pressed each into working for somebody else, their levels of happiness and growth have varied because of other choices, including the way each chose to see himself or herself.

•••

*George G., retired senior executive, multinational corporation.*

Ten years earlier, George had left his uncle's company as a vice president, doubting his ability and success. Now, he returned from a failed venture at a much lower position. And it was there, in retrospect, where he should have stayed. "The happiest years of my life: I wasn't a manager."

But society (and George's own personal sense of success) did not acknowledge achievement as anything but upward mobility and increased income. Wherever the company pushed him, up he went. Making any other choice was too frightening.

"I think choices represent a scary idea. I expect I'm almost the type of person who requires structure, who should have stayed in the Armed Forces for thirty years. I don't really want to be this way. But it's scary to think about doing something else."

Because George didn't choose something else, his retirement now feels tight, distressed, empty. In the first chapter, he candidly shared how fear of failure was keeping him from fully exploring his artistic abilities. A narrow focus in past choices seems to have also created an even narrower retirement. When one's nose remains plastered to the grindstone, other areas and interests aren't even glimpsed peripherally.

I truly celebrate George's ability to verbalize for others what he is just now beginning to discover for himself. His candor helps all of us. And by honestly looking at what has been, he can—if he chooses—begin to regain the balance in the neglected areas of his life.

For Sandy R., the move from elementary education into selling industrial couplings, has precipitated balance in some areas and imbalance in others. "Sailing" is difficult at times.

•••

*Sandy R., traveling sales representative.*

Before leaving the teaching profession permanently, Sandy had taken a year's sabbatical to develop a teaching module for the U.S. Senate Computer Center. Although offered a management position, she returned to teaching because she missed her friends and the children.

The need for a more substantial income became a great concern. The second—the need for love. "In teaching, I was substituting a relationship with the kids for a relationship with a man. I was giving it all away because I wasn't emotionally tied to anyone." She turned to an employment counselor as a way to find an alternative to teaching.

Besides income, the "job" has brought some internal problems." I think teaching was a shelter. When I was a teacher, I doubted my ability to do anything else. Teaching was a way to quickly lose self-confidence with adults and the ability to work with peers. When the employment counselor found this job, I was intrigued but scared. Now I know I can drive up to an oil refinery. I can read mechanical drawings. I know I'm responsible for the accounts I bring in."

"If I ever get in a position where I want to leave, I can go off and search for adventure. At least now I have a choice. Although this job is hard, teaching was harder on the emotions. My sales manager had first said that he would never hire a woman. But we worked and grew together, which resulted in my being above quota every quarter."

But there are imbalances along the way. Her perfectionism as a teacher has translated into long hours, lots of travel. "I feel like there's not enough of me to go around. Sometimes I unplug my phone and read a book. Now, I've got this unknown virus which has lasted for months: headaches, constant exhaustion, and a low-grade fever. But I don't think it's job related."

When asked about teaching, Sandy's eyes begin to brim with tears, much to her surprise. "I will never do anything that will give me the sense of satisfaction that I had with teaching. What an impact: you can make or break a child; either destroy or build their self-confidence. I didn't realize [in reference to her tears] how much I had invested with them. I miss them."

Amazing, isn't it, what we can learn about ourselves through choices. For all the apparent dilemma of balance which Sandy is beginning to realize, her outlook allows her to be flexible with herself and, therefore, to alter course. "Change is growth. Anytime you move into the unknown, you grow. The more self-knowledge, the more you have to give. Allowing yourself the opportunity to grow in business and personally is the only way you can say, 'This is who I am,'" adds Sandy.

During the year's exploration which preceded her entry into an educational-equipment company, Ronda S. carefully considered all of the areas which were out of balance and just how a work setting would need to be structured in order to challenge and excite her.

•••

*Ronda S., sales representative.*

"As a speech therapist, I was always working on someone who needed to be 'fixed.' I wondered what it would be like to be creative and cause a change in other people's lives. I knew I liked to be with people in a creative rather than regimented setting. I needed to be in charge, make decisions. I also like the idea of bringing together friends from different environments, putting together different pieces of information, being a central networker."

When she sold her house and moved to another city to be with her boyfriend, financial and emotional stability increased. She knew that whatever work she found, there would have to be time allowed for him, enough income to support her needs, and time for exercise and church attendance.

"What I found is a blend of education with technology. I can set my own time and I move to people rather than them coming to me. My clients are all school districts. I not only understand but can have sympathy for their paperwork, as well as financial burdens. And I am finding lots of ways to be creative with new applications for the equipment every day. I am also able to put people together so they can collaborate on the use of the equipment and learn from each other. As for balance, I am still missing the ingredient of really 'making a difference' so I might make it up with some volunteer work. I don't want material things to take precedence."

## The Integration Move

When we think of someone "closing up shop" to return to work for someone else, the more common response is to think, "Well, they just couldn't make enough money at it." Pretty fair assumption. But there are other reasons behind such a decision.

•••

*Paul O. (fictitious name), former real estate sales executive, now escrow agent.*

For five years, Paul had worked hard building up a real-estate business in San Francisco. He spent weekends taking clients around, met with other agents during the evenings, and always found his telephone answering machine filled with calls whenever he went away. Financially, life was fine. But he wasn't.

"It was crazy. I never had enough time for me. Or for that matter, even enough time to develop a significant relationship."

When he was 36, Paul stopped making deals. He accepted a nine-to-five job with an hourly salary at a small escrow company. "I got my life back. I moved into a tiny apartment, which simplified everything from cleaning to the quantity of furniture. I began taking evening classes just for the heck of it. I read books. I took up camping. I basically started to enjoy my life."

As for money, Paul made an interesting discovery. "I had always worried about money. You know, having enough to get what I wanted, make payments and all that jazz. As soon as I decided to stop worrying about money, I have always had enough!! Not an overabundance, mind you, but always enough. That's sure better than worrying!"

## The Sit-Tight Move

Although at first glance, this might sound like a contradiction, another choice for work/balance/living might be to stay exactly where you are (provided you are happy), while at the same time making plans for a new growth pattern. It might be that the time is coming when a "road not taken" will become the chosen path. Retirement might be in the offing or a dormant interest might flower. Whatever the reason, I believe it is not only healthy but vital that we maintain growth in numerous areas of interest.

Case in point: Few would deny the fact that Charles is a very good lawyer. The law firm considers him an asset and there's a good working relationship with his colleagues. But Charles has a passion: writing music. Now that he no longer has to "prove" himself and take tricky cases, there's time for his music. He has started taking classes in music writing, attending seminars, and playing the piano more frequently. His goal at some time: leave the firm and do nothing but write music.

•••

*Daryl P., (fictitious name) director of public works for one of the fastest-growing metropolitan cities in the nation.*

Daryl has a grip like a bear and a hand just about as big. The massive deer's head hanging on his office wall attests to the fact that he is every bit the hunter he claims to be.

"It's my avocation. I love hunting and fishing. In fact, that's how I became a civil engineer. I had a summer job surveying in the mountains and discovered that I could end a day's work and head to the woods."

He's also uncovered a gift for patience and humor. Handling any city job with its attendant political turmoil, the rush of steady development, and a staff of 160, demands the same skill as waiting in a duck blind. "Some things you just have to wait out," he chuckles, "and if you relax, stay calm, the problems often resolve themselves."

Throughout his decade-plus career with the city, Daryl has also made sure that he creates balance for both the avocation as well as his family. "Instead of taking the first raise I was offered, I asked for more time off. Now I've got plenty built up and can head up to our ranch retreat or just off to nearby game preserves. Sometimes alone, sometimes with family, sometimes with my friends."

Life is fine. But Daryl has a dream. "I'd like to make this even more pleasurable. When the kids are gone, we're thinking about spending six months here and maybe six months at the ranch. I'd like to do consulting in advocacy or planning. But when we head to the ranch, maybe I can put together hunting trips for a fee. Right now, my wife and I are just exploring."

Driving up the freeway one evening during this past Christmas season, I was startled to see a long row of Christmas lights floating at what seemed to be sixty feet in mid-air. "What the heck," I muttered squinting through the dusty windshield. Finally, I approached the lights glowing at the end of an empty tract of land. Now illuminated by street lamps, I realized that the colored lights were not performing some trick in levitation. They were strung along the boom of a gigantic construction crane crouched beside the foundation of a new high-rise. Even in the midst of ordinary, daily labor, someone had decided that the piece of machinery should participate in the holiday celebration!

Can we humans expect less from our daily labor? Making choices for moving around a company, or into one, or—as we'll read in a minute—out of one and into our own, is part of our need to celebrate. We don't want to feel left out of any of the joy which might be ours to claim. But nobody can do it for us. Maybe that's why there were also plenty of other construction cranes with dark colorless booms sitting in solemn silence throughout that holiday season. I think they were waiting.

## The Entrepreneurial Choice

"Get out on a limb. That's where the fruit is." I have no idea what Will Rogers had in mind when he made this statement, but it certainly applies to the mind-set of an entrepreneur, the self-employed individual. Of course, there are as many different kinds of "fruit" as there are "limbs."

Probably the number one golden apple is independence, the ability to answer to no one but yourself. This can be a large misconception. Depending upon the nature of your work, Uncle Sam, labor unions, EEO boards and public agencies dictate much of your life. When you are the "boss" (even if you boss only yourself), the work can be both your master and mistress, your slave driver and lover. It all depends upon your choices for balance as to who does most of the driving.

For this reason, I think the healthiest way to look at the "independence" fruit is that it first feeds your giftedness and quality of life. Note that I did not say independence "increases your income, lets you take vacations more often and means you don't have to deal with irritating people and egos."

The reality is that despite the enormous starts in new businesses, the majority will fail within the first two years. The reality is that it could well take three or more years before you might be able to even live off your income much less make a profit. The reality is that whether you offer a service or product, people become your primary concern. If you don't deal with the customer or client directly, you'll still have to effectively manage the other people who will.

This doesn't mean don't follow your dream. But it does mean make your choices wisely. As long as you focus on using your talents and interests, you're off to a good start. A false start is getting into something different "just because." There are plenty of good books, courses, and consultants who will tell you the prerequisites for an enterprise: prior experience or the willingness to go through training; an analysis of the marketplace and competitors; management skills; accurate financial assessment and budgeting; and a well-conceived marketing plan.

But in this book, my concern is that you consider why you make the choice, what impact it will have on the quality of your life, and how you structure that "work" along with other equally important decisions in life.

For example, an entrepreneurial decision might come from lifestyle considerations. A financial analyst from Los Angeles opened a ski shop in the mountains of Vermont and gained back the family he had ignored. By the same token, the company president who refused to adjust lifestyle requirements and take less than her $6,000 per month salary out of her business ended up losing it.

Ah, the interconnectedness of choices!

Consider this: While waiting for the arrival of her third baby, a housewife who loved to sew accessories for the baby's room discovered a need for her giftedness. Now, seven children later and with a portfolio of everything from wall hangings to baby crib bumpers, she has a multimillion-dollar manufacturing company. She's discovered other talents and is ready to spread her wings in new directions, with the same husband of long ago. By the same token, a colleague recently told me about a woman who owns a quite unique gift store but runs herself and the family ragged. "She's great at what she does; she's shattered by how she does it."

Ah, balance.

Or an entrepreneurial decision might rest in the ability to continue the same line of work but at a different pace and setting. Sean F., the once-burned-out cameraman for ABC and former photographer for the California Angels, has now created a new line of work with challenge and excitement: video productions concerning nature. "We've filmed bass-fishing tournaments, snowmobiling and ice fishing, and completed a feature on river steelhead. As of today, our Outdoor News Network show is scheduled to be broadcast over the Satellite Programming Network (SPN) within the next few months. We climb mountains now to get pictures. And we like to incorporate the human spirit within the beauty of the natural surroundings. I can pick projects and be discriminating because our overhead is very slim."

On the flip side of the coin, a former Los Angeles Times still photographer who captured history-making photos of presidents, astronauts, and even wayward animals now has a video-production corporation and studio for filming corporate-programming documentaries and commercials. His state-of-the-art facility requires a different pace and harmony. "Our projects use a multitude of ideas, from a multitude of people, with sophisticated hardware, all of which is filtered into a complete production on site."

Both entrepreneurs, similar choices, different balances in work setting. Vive le difference.

There is one advance warning. If entrepreneurial adventure occurs as a mid-life career switch, be prepared to make alterations in the way you sail through life. According to Fortune magazine, "The second-careerist's biggest problem might seem to be maintaining his or her accustomed standard of living. Incomes tend to be low, often no more than one-third the annual compensation of the first career."

## A Word About Families

Can you imagine what trouble a quarterback would have if he tried to make a touchdown without first going into a huddle with his teammates? Some might get mad and storm off the field. Others might try and play, but not knowing the game plan they would become confused and would be of zero help.

The same thing can happen with a family. Recall the medical researcher who was surprised to find out that his wife actually wanted him to seek what basically amounted to a demotion. If he had talked with her about his feelings and she had candidly shared back, the dilemma of staying in a management position might not have lasted so long.

Because a change in one area of your life impacts a change in all, dialogue is necessary. Particularly if there are children. For one thing, children fear change unless (like anyone else) they know what to expect and what role they play in that change. Even an absence of job titles can leave a child bewildered. Surprisingly, children have also learned (at way too early an age) to worry about money.

I recently met a divorced woman with a teen-aged son. When 40-plus-year-old Mom decided to leave her job as principal and seek other avenues of personal growth, her son was upset.

"I later learned that he loved telling the other kids that his mom was a principal. Without a title (I'm a management consultant), he didn't know what I did. And he was afraid we would have to move from our house." Open conversation has handled that concern, and Mom is on to more risking and growing.

The more a family can be involved in the decision-making process, even if it is in just understanding a parent's thoughts and feelings behind potential choices, there can indeed be two-way support.

A friend of mine recently left a well-paying position with a national public-relations firm to start a monthly newsletter and to handle his own roster of clients. The entire family became involved in the change. They did everything from stuffing envelopes, to cleaning out the garage for his new office, to covering the phone. By playing quarterback, he's got a family team rooting for his latest adventure in growing.

Of course, let me complete this story. Before beginning his new direction, my friend played "mother" so that his wife could complete her later-in-life degree and become a CPA. Now, it's his turn.

Honest communication which leads to teamwork is the touchdown skill.

## In Considering the Eeney, Meeney, Miney, Mo

Henry Ford is credited with proclaiming, "You can't build a reputation on what you're going to do." He's right. You can't claim any freedom to live unless you lead the charge into change, monitoring balance all the while.

Additionally, there is also validity in the ancient Orthodox Jewish axiom which claims, "The gift without the giver is bare." This implies that a giver of a gift has to use it first before handing it away. The giver first cooks in the pot; first wears a shawl. Only then comes the gift-giving. Otherwise, there is nothing of the giver within the gift. It is empty.

The same thing is true of both our "work" or our "job." If we give only the minimum which is required, we'll probably get just the minimum back. The effort, therefore, is not in the quantity of our work but in the quality in which it is done and the spirit in which it is given.

By the same token, we have every right to expect reciprocation. But sometimes we've got to ask for it.

Paula works for a company that assigns clients to their respective employees. Since she has been with the firm, it has grown by leaps and bounds, literally doubling its income within two months, but adding only one new person and not hiring temporaries during vacation times.

Paula feels personally responsible for the paperwork she handles for clients and has worked weekends and nights to keep up the volume. "I suddenly realized that I was doing all the giving and not receiving anything in return. I realized that I had to speak up, stand on the quality of my work, and just see where the cards fell. I had to do it for me."

Mustering up courage, she wrote a letter, explaining her perception of the situation and unwillingness to accept such a shortage of staff. "The manager and owner walked on tiptoe after my letter, complimented my work, gave me a raise, and hired another person. That was more than I had expected! Sure it was a gamble, but now I really know that the quality of my work has paid off."

In the last three chapters, we'll look at some instances where change in the work/job picture has been forced upon individuals and how they have handled it, what are the common mental/emotional ups and downs which we all face in our growing, and lastly, how do we celebrate and live today.

## Summary

1. Although multiple choices can be frightening, there are two more concepts which might provide a more well-rounded sample of possible decisions:

- Creativity encourages you to see connections and possibilities for your work or job beyond what is a traditional path.

- The "Road Not Taken" encourages you to consider walking a "path" which for some reason in the past was not taken.


2. The Corporate Choice can be considered with these options:

Moving around on the inside:

- Lateral Move (for growth of skill or a similar but different department)

- Enrichment Move (to make your current job better)

- Exploratory Move (to try totally different fields and new skills within the same company)

- Realignment Move (to elect a downward path for more balance and personal satisfaction)

- Relocation Move (to seek work in another company or as an entrepreneur)

- Vertical Move (to advance to a higher position and salary)

Moving in from the outside might be considered for financial security or for balance.

The Sit-Tight Move encourages enjoyment of current position while at the same time allows oneself to explore other interests for another time.


3. Entrepreneurial Choice:

In all cases, feed your giftedness first and heed the wisdom of those who have gone before.


4. Before making a substantial choice, create a family team by opening communication channels.

# Chapter Eight
# The Timely Tragedy

---

*Sorrow comes to make room in the heart for joy.*

*– The prophet, Kahlil Gibran*

---

"I know a boy who grew seven inches in one year," declared a visiting friend when I was complaining about the futility of buying shoes for a growing adolescent. Noting my disbelief, she continued.

"It's true. His mother told me that one morning her son came out for breakfast complaining that he hurt all ove—every joint and every muscle. He claimed he knew it was because he had grown overnight. Since his mom had measured him just the day before on a height chart hung on the inside of the linen closet door, they repeated the procedure. Sure enough—a new half an inch!"

I didn't really care whether my friend exaggerated or not. The part of the story which struck a responsive chord in me was that the boy hurt when he grew. And the more hurt, the faster the growth.

There is no joy in being fired, going through a divorce, experiencing the death of a loved one, declaring bankruptcy, or suffering from serious illness. There is no happiness with deep disappointment or the agony of defeat. But there is tremendous opportunity for personal growth amid the pain.

From my experience, as well as from the many people who have shared their stories, I'm convinced that such painful growing inevitably produces a fuller realization of giftedness and a more intense appreciation of living. But there is a catch. One must acknowledge, work through, and step out of that pain by actively making choices for positive growth. Otherwise, bitterness, self-pity, and eventual stagnation are the results.

I really felt a deep commitment to include this chapter. The truth of the matter is that sometimes we aren't in a "pit" until the onslaught of a seemingly terrible event that kicks us out of the proverbial catbird seat. In other instances, we might be aware of an unhappy or imbalanced work/life but we don't spring into action until we're forced to. If there was ever a time when you needed to know that others had indeed passed through and triumphed, it is now. Hence this chapter.

Were it not for a budget cut and two months' severance pay, Cheryl's dream of working as a freelance writer and creating fiction stories would have had reality only in midnight slumber. Were it not for the cancellation of his English teaching job and the discovery that his separated wife had a new beau, William Least Heat Moon would never have traveled those forgotten American roads and produced his best-seller Blue Highways. Charles D.'s catalyst for finally walking away from his company came because he watched his father die. "I realized that he had never had any fun or time off in his life. I didn't want my life to end like that." Even broadcaster/author Studs Terkel observed that were it not for a lucky set of circumstances, he would have been an admittedly unhappy lawyer. He flunked the bar exam.

Although each probably entered a state of depression or at least a blue funk over the event, none of them remained there. When one door closed, they chose to open another. Sometimes, one doesn't even know what's on the other side of the new door. Case in point:

Many years ago, my then-soon-to-be husband invested considerable money and time into seeking a contract which would have moved us out of the state. I was ecstatic because if he won the contract, I was to leave my job as a senior account executive with a public-relations firm and become the director of communications for a 200-person project. What a challenge! What an opportunity to put together everything from written materials to employee-relations programs!

A week after we were married, word came back. "Sorry. You didn't make it." The door which we had both dreamed about slammed shut with the finality of a bank vault. Only I had my foot caught.

It took but a few weeks of deep depression, frustration, headaches and tears to realize that I had been using Bill's project as a way to get out of a situation which no longer matched the "me" I was becoming. Instead of making a choice for myself, I had tried to let "circumstance" do it for me.

And our circumstances seemed sticky: three stepchildren soon to be living with us, Bill's consulting work in a slump from his single devotion to the contract proposal, and a "pit" for me. At face value, the resultant downside from the risk of seeking the contract looked too steep.

Yet with Bill's encouragement, I left the secure world of a monthly paycheck. Today, thanks to that timely tragedy, I am beginning to discover giftedness which I never knew I had. And he has developed a management concept unique to his profession.

## You've Been Fired

When you read the heading of this section, do you wince? Feel ill at ease? I did. Just those words alone are a real downer. The connotation behind "getting fired," whether it's for budget cutbacks or just plain unsuitability for the job, is that you are not worthy. The downsizing of the last half of this decade has reached record numbers. In the scheme of things, you can be replaced. And the higher up in salary and rank, the more traumatic the termination.

Turning the traumatic into opportunity is what Bill E. knows best.

"When I was 42, I got lucky. I was fired." Now sitting in his office years after that timely tragedy, Bill references the unfolding process in his "work," the resultant success of his company, and what his clients have discovered about themselves.

"I was vice president of personnel for a major transportation carrier at the time I was asked to leave. But for some time I realized that the title really should have been 'labor relations.' I was the classic case of the misfit."

The company gave him five months to look at what he wanted, "and for the first time in my lie, that's exactly what I did."

"With the help of a process supplied by some consultants, I looked at myself and discovered things I never considered before. First, since about the age of 10, it seems like I have been a natural counselor for my family, for school friends, and for my colleagues at work. Counseling is a streak that runs through my life like a thread."

"The second thing I found out was that I was something of a performer. I liked to get up before a group. I never did stand-up presentations in my work, but the talent was there on the inside. I also realized that I had the ability to put myself in the other guy's shoes, to have empathy.

"What this showed me was that my skills were dealing on a one-to-one basis with others. The top job in personnel within the corporation involves managing, planning, and organizing—taking me away from what I was best at doing. My skills are interpersonal, performing, training, and speaking.

"Half of me said 'Go out on your own.' The other half said 'What, are you kidding? After twenty years of getting a paycheck!'

"But that's what I did; I didn't know what my inherent skills were until I was 42 years old. I also discovered that I was a risk-taker and that I like change. So here I am."

According to Bill, the average profile of the outplaced executive whom he counsels is a 46-year-old executive. The corporate reason for firing the executive might be one or all of the following:

1. A misfit. (This is a talented person who just gets into the wrong kind of job.)

2. Personality clash. (A new man or woman who regularly runs into conflict with senior management.)

3. Economic cutbacks.

4. The Redundant Executive. (The man or woman has moved ahead into a position that really carries no definition or responsibility. And there they stay as a figurehead.)

5. "Downsizing" to meet global competition.

Regardless of the corporate rationale, Bill has discovered that all of his displaced executives were really unhappy to begin with.

"I don't think there is anyone who has come in to see us who didn't have some sense of being miserable in his or her job. That's why getting fired can really be the key to opportunity. Many people don't like what they are doing but won't make an effort to change because they like getting the paycheck ... they don't want to ripple the waters. They're in neutral, without vibrancy, just coasting. Many just think about it through their entire careers. Some are so anxious about their job insecurity, they've become immobile and have not taken responsibility for their own careers. I've done retirement counseling and heard people say, 'Well, this is what I've done and I really hated it but the social aspects (lunches, friends, etc.) kept me going."

"Sure you hear a lot about middle managers getting axed and how tragic it is. But in many ways, that's going to change their lives in a positive way. Most people don't want to look at themselves, to open the door. But when you're fired, you're forced to. You have to take responsibility for yourself. The crutch is gone."

In looking back over their achievements and what energized them, the terminated executives learn how to talk about themselves and what skills they bring to the world.

"People get defined according to their jobs and job descriptions are very narrow. Even if someone doesn't like being an engineer, ask who they are and they'll say 'an engineer.' So very early on, you get a label and don't know that it's just an invisible piece of paper that can come off at will. You don't know that you have tremendous powers and abilities far bigger than any job."

Once realization of inherent abilities sets in—even if triggered by losing a job—the process of unfolding must continue. Bill admits he's feeling the tug of still-untapped skills. "I feel like I'm moving toward more speaking, performing, and seminars. There is much information which I can share."

## When the Spouse Has Gone

I have to place the blame at the feet of society for what I am about to write. I didn't make it up. It's a matter of sociological happenstance: Divorce or the death of a spouse carries more severe impact in the work/job arena for women than for men.

Of all the divorced people you know, how many women have received such a gracious settlement that they do not have to work? Not very many out of the total picture, hmm? And yet, how many of those women (1) never had a job, (2) have a job but with a salary much lower than the former husband, (3) have custody of the children.

Now think about divorced men and answer those same questions, substituting the word "wife" for "husband" in question two. Do you see the difference?

I had to ask myself these questions when I began compiling case studies for this chapter. As I searched and asked for potential people to interview, it appeared that more men grew in their "work" through the tragedy of job termination whereas more women grew in their "work" through divorce or death of a spouse.

The Bureau of Labor Statistics confirmed at least part of my supposition: men's income after divorce rose whereas women's income declined.

Sure, there are exceptions. I personally know of one case where the ex-wife took the husband to the cleaners and he is faced with starting all over again from scratch. And, thankfully, there is a slow and good change in the court philosophy which has more equitably divided the responsibility for child-rearing.

But in general, you can see why more divorced or widowed women would have a greater likelihood to encounter "work" with more trauma than men. And if a woman has never worked, hopefully you can appreciate her tremendous difficulty and therefore potential in discovering her giftedness.

At The Women's Opportunity Center on the University of California campus in Irvine, thousands have availed themselves to this non-profit prototype career and personal counseling service.

According to a former director, "A number of the women we have seen are the products of an affluent life. They've been married to movers and shakers, contenting themselves with a 'devoted wife' role. Suddenly, they're left without an identity, and frequently, without much income. They see themselves as unskilled, incapable, and futureless. We assist them in going through a process to identify and tap hidden knowledge and skills. I can readily say that most of our clients discover potential which they never thought they had. Now divorce has become the best thing in the world for them."

A few examples: One divorcee is a well-known former actress in her 50s. She never completed high school and has always been surrounded by servants. Now faced with a much different future, she's returning to get her degree and is getting excited over new possibilities.

On the other end of the spectrum, another woman lost everything, including a place to stay. She slept in her station wagon. When she'd came into the Center's Job Seekers Clinic, they always were surprised to see how professionally dressed she appeared. Someone complimented her clothing, only to learn that each outfit had been carefully orchestrated with penny-pinching wisdom from a local thrift store. The important point here is that she began to reframe the way she saw herself. She now found a good job working with doctors.

Sometimes, the divorced or widowed woman must unfold gradually. When Joyce (fictitious name) entered the doors of the Job Seekers Clinic she could not give a positive statement about herself. Her self-esteem was down the drain and her skills (to her way of thinking) were negligible. A series of smaller jobs began to boost her confidence and allow her to discover more about herself. Today, she's one of the top sales representatives for a manufacturer of pharmaceutical supplies.

Not all women, or men for that matter, have such resources as the Center available to them. But even without that assistance, those who successfully move through divorce and into a growing work/life balance have managed to first tap into their giftedness. Although both women in the following case studies started their personal journeys with divorces, their stories contain universal messages about risk and gain and "work."

•••

*Marsha P. (fictitious name), director of a private pre-school and elementary school.*

When she's on the playground with her 3-year-old students, Marsha moves to a different beat. She's no longer 47 years old with three almost grown-up sons, but a youngster—giggling, playing ball, pretending.

There are 250 children in her school and she knows each by name. It's easy when teaching and loving children for their special individuality is a heartfelt philosophy.

But Marsha almost kept that gift under wraps. "Although I taught five years before my first son was born, I quit as soon as he came. The culture said that a good wife and mother didn't work. That's what I believed in. So instead, I helped Tom get his business started. I even wrote his dissertation for him."

For thirteen years, Marsha played at housewife, mother and father. More often than not, Tom traveled during the week and was too tired to notice either his sons or his wife.

"I really wanted to get back with children and other adults. Tom didn't know it, and wouldn't have approved, but I volunteered for an inner-city Head Start program where I could take my boys along with me. They were the only towheads in the group!"

The older Marsha got, the more unhappy she became. Tom told her that she was being foolish to ask for repeated signs of affection and more "at home time."

Finally, at the age of 36, her marriage had deteriorated to such a state that Tom, in a fit of anger, threw Marsha and the boys out of the house.

"What a scary, frightening experience. For two weeks, the boys and I lived in a motel until I could find a job at a pre-school. I could take the two youngest with me and drop my other son at elementary school. Tom refused to give me any money and the job provided just enough for a small apartment and food for us."

Although her husband finally relented and allowed them to return, the marriage was over." I accepted a position as the director of a church-related school in order to be home when the boys got out of school. It was like having your cake and eating it too."

Having subsequently enrolled in a masters program at a university in the next county, Marsha continued to refine her teaching skills and philosophy. "I realized that the idea of mainstreaming special-needs children within a regular classroom was something that could not wait until elementary school. But when I tried it at the church school, the board members balked."

Up against a wall, Marsha took a deep breath, sold her share of stock from the divorce settlement, and started a private school where she could provide more individualized learning and encourage early admittance of youngsters with disabilities.

That was nineteen years ago. Today, the school that started with forty-five preschoolers now goes up to grade six and the woman who had never thought further than marriage and babies now deals with corporate board members, employees, and accountants. "And I got my degree, even if it took me seven years and a 100-mile round-trip commute."

There's a man back in her life, whitewater raft trips, aerobics classes, a bevy of friends from all walks of life, and an avid interest in holistic health. Recently, she sold the school to start another career.

Do you remember Sunny F., the woman from Chapter One who headed out to California with her teen-aged daughter, $1,500 to her name, and a "maybe" job in the wings? Seven years later, at age 54, her writing started to roll: a book on archery for the Olympics; a script sold to network television; teachers' guides and filmstrips for Disney; a radio telethon for a national charity campaign; a teleconference script on agriculture for a bank in the Midwest; and a movie-of-the-week script currently under consideration. Quite an accomplishment for a lady who didn't begin unfolding until the end of a twenty-year marriage.

•••

*Sunny, F., writer for business, industry, and television.*

"Leaving my marriage, at the age of 42, was the first time I ever took control of my life. Ever. Up until then I had allowed myself to be pushed and manipulated into everything. My life had always been in other people's hands because I had to please everyone. I had to be loved and the only way to be loved was to be the person everyone wants you to be. I got so lost in being a person for someone else, I never found out who I was.

"Deciding to seek a divorce was the most painful decision. I had what I called a mini-breakdown, crying at the tiniest things all the time. Things were happening in my life which I would ignore until I became physically sick. There was no one I could talk to because everyone thought I had a perfect marriage; I was the perfect wife, the perfect mother. When the doctor couldn't find a damn thing wrong with me, I got scared and realized I had to make a decision.

"I started writing because I could do it at home and be a good mother. We really needed the money.

"Wherever we had moved in the past, I would call on public relations and advertising agencies even though at first I hadn't done that type of writing. My college degree is in speech therapy."

But Sunny was scared. "I didn't really believe in my own talent or ability. Confidence level was zero. I never thought of myself as being able to be really good at writing. At that time in my life, I knew I loved to write but...."

Within short order, another crisis. The production company closed its doors, the little money she had was gone, a daughter still had to be fed and there were no jobs in the small town.

When there's no road in sight, some people seek counselors. Sunny sought a psychic. "She insisted that I was going to work at a university in the northern part of the state—a crazy notion since I don't have a masters—and go back to school. I told her that was ridiculous. I didn't have two cents and what money I did have for school was to help my daughter with college."

In less than a week, a casual acquaintance called to ask if she would consider applying for an adjunct teaching position in a university school of journalism!

"I didn't have any journalism training, though I had done a house magazine for a national hamburger chain. I knew nothing about printing and yet there I was, talking to the dean of the school. I had never taught, but I knew I would love it; daydreamed about it. But without a masters, it all seemed so impossible."

The impossible did occur. When the dean heard about her background in film, Sunny was sent directly to the chairman of the broadcasting department who also served as the general manager of the university's public television station. A $9,000-per-year job was available doing public relations for the station. "I knew I couldn't live on that, but what choice did I have?"

After a two-hour interview, the chairman became her mentor. "He tore up the application from another person and sent me down to apply for the public-relations job. He also told me to hang loose about a part-time teaching position.

Patience paid off. He got a waiver for her to teach despite the missing master's degree. On and off for the next three years she taught, learning just ahead of the students. "I was asked to take over a news-writing lab. Never having written that format, I studied the material and taught the lab. A student was sent to me so that I could teach her how to write a screenplay. So I learned how to write a screenplay."

While teaching the news-writing lab, a documentary film on a Presbyterian hunger project sent her to Bangladesh. (She had done a similar project in Brazil a few years earlier.)

"Up until that time, I still didn't believe I was really any good. I didn't believe I had value. But I found myself halfway across the world and loving every minute of it. People's reaction when they heard of my work convinced me—not because the film was the greatest, but because I had been called twice to go overseas. That says something. I was not just getting these things because I was cheap and needed the money. People were beginning to treat me with respect. It changed my attitude about myself."

It was then that Sunny decided she wanted to be a star ... "and that I always wanted to be a star ever since I was growing up. I remember being on stage toe dancing, music playing, and people applauding. I loved it, simply loved it.

"This 'stardom' I wanted now was not being in the spotlight, but being recognized for my craft. Being so good that people will use my name in reference to good writers. At age 45, that all became rekindled. I didn't just want to be a college professor and survive. I wanted to be such a damn successful writer that I'd be invited back to teach, maybe even awarded an honorary doctorate. I love working with talent and pulling it out, but I didn't want to be a news teacher doing the same course year after year. With all my heart and soul I wanted to do dramatic writing."

It hasn't been easy. The risks remain but the giftedness that began unfolding with a divorce has attracted a sense of happiness and well-being.

"When I look back, I don't even know who that woman is from my past life. I felt like a caterpillar until I went to the university. Then I became a butterfly. It gave me a chance to find out that I could make it on my own after twenty years. It built courage. Before then, I was never fully me. I did a lot of nice things, even wrote a musical which was very successful, but I never related those things to who I was. Now I relate who I am to what I do."

## You've Lost Your Business

Some married friends of ours are currently engaged in a critical struggle to keep open what once was a very profitable company that rebuilt engines for trucks. Unexpected debt from buying out a partner, a too-soon expansion move, and poor management has placed them in a position where Chapter 11 bankruptcy might be the only solution.

"So if that's what happens, and we sell the house, we'll still be all right. We've got each other and our health." With an attitude like that and some of the fine help they've acquired, they are confident that they'll make it. But some people aren't so lucky.

When losing a business does strike, two opportunities can result from the tragedy. The first is balance and a resetting of priorities. Not infrequently, an enterprise fails because too much money was taken out of the business to handle choices in other life areas or too little attention was paid to the business of management. In these cases, a "clean slate" might allow an individual to reorganize "living" and "working" in a more manageable fashion. Ultimately, that must be a plus.

But the greater opportunity which might lay buried underneath such a tragedy is a newfound freedom to really explore and find one's true "work." In this trial-and-error process of figuring out just who we are and how we want to be, there's a pretty good chance that the lost business is merely a detour in our journey.

•••

Such was the case with Martin W. (fictitious name), who at the time I first met him, was president of a graphic design studio with gross annual billings *around $600,000.*

When I first walked into Martin's graphic design studio, this boyish-looking commercial artist was completing the final touches on a packaging idea for a pharmaceutical house. Three other employees seemed intently involved in their specific assignments for a stable of clients which included a large biomedical firm and an auto manufacturer. Wife Susan manned the reception desk, waiting until it was time to go home to their two children.

At first glance, it appeared like any other graphic studio. Until, that is, Martin gave me a tour.

Behind his desk on the second floor was a small door. When I inquired as to that space, Martin allowed me to enter a room under the eaves of the building. A great winged owl glared at me from its rough pine-tree perch; deer nuzzled gentle spring grass; and a massive gray whale glided through watery light filtered between bands of blue-green crystal and velvet. All as alive as if I were the original Creator. All captured within a world no bigger than a picture frame.

Martin's business sign might have read "commercial artist" but here was his true gift—fine-arts illustration of wildlife.

"But why aren't you doing this," I gasped reaching out to touch the paper, feel the paint, and make sure that it wasn't a very artistic photograph. "Too busy," answered Martin, hurrying into the next room but not before he sighed. "I work on this at home in the garage but I rarely have the time. I don't have the credentials to do this for a living.

"Commercial art supports us."

End of conversation. And after three months, end of the project which had mutually used our skills. I heard no more from Martin for almost three years until the bottom fell out and he called me.

"I always felt rather inept at running the business. I couldn't manage people very well and I'm afraid it was easy for Sue and I to be taken advantage of. We were talked into incorporating more as a protection against personal liability since we handled drug and medical accounts. However, unknown to us, the accountant continued to file our tax return as if we were sole proprietors."

Martin didn't know about the error until a state tax official walked up the driveway to his home and handed him a bill for some $8,000 in unpaid corporate taxes and penalties. The agency agreed to accept an initial minimum payment of $1,000 per week for eight weeks. (Later, the IRS requirement would bring the total amount to almost $32,000!)

"We scrambled like hell and immediately sold what we could. But now there was an even bigger nut to crack. A graphic designer has heavy out-of-pocket expenses until the client can be billed. We sold some of the office furniture and cut back on employees."

When the fourth week came around, Martin missed the payment deadline by one day. The state tax agency instantly seized all personal accounts. "Only later did we learn that the agency acted improperly but that it would take more money and probably four years to handle any litigation. Besides, on that day—it made little difference.

"Our house payment was due and the only money we had was in my pocket and Sue's purse. That same day, a letter arrived from a major client on retainer, picking up on the 30-day cancellation clause in the contract."

Susan went back to work as an office manager for a doctor. Martin closed shop and moved his commercial art home. "We lived off of everything in the pantry while I used the checks from clients to pay bills. I pounded the streets, hit and miss. It felt like a giant roller coaster. I'd get enough work to support the family and then, whoosh! Down in the valley."

In retrospect, the valley created by this tragedy provided Martin with the time and drive to unleash his creative genius. "I painted my brains out and spent much of the time meeting the scientific community, museum curators, marine biologists, and ornithologists. I even met with a major environmental group and had a whale painting ready to be turned into a poster when the funding was cut."

To earn more money, Martin located a gallery specializing in wildlife. Though the interior of the gallery provided a gorgeous backdrop for his work, its location next to a shopping center proved disastrous.

"But through the gallery, I met other wildlife artists. One of them, who was among the original members of Greenpeace, invited me to display my work at the Mendocino County Whale Festival in Northern California.

"After having my ego take such a blow, wondering how I could have been so stupid to have fallen into the trap of the big office, I felt reconfirmed by the Mendocino artists. One artist whom I had read so much about and greatly admired came to my display at the festival. He stood for over an hour looking at my work like a kid in a candy store—the same way I felt about his talent. The next day, he returned with a camera and asked permission to photograph it."

At the end of one week in Mendocino County, Susan and Martin looked at each other, thought about the metropolitan rat race and said, "Why not! We're selling our house to pay the state, and the IRS will soon be along. Rent is cheaper in this area but most of all, there are people here who will help support my work. They're our kind—real people without pretense and show. Considering the fact that I sold a number of paintings during the festival, it seems that the area is also visited by people who appreciate wildlife artistry."

The wheels are now in motion for such a move and a new life. All because of a seeming tragedy.

## A Potpourri of Misfortune

I have purposely selected those timely tragedies which appear to have universal recognition for many of us. This doesn't exclude the fact there may be any number of events which hit us below the belt, force us into action, and encourage a rethinking of our personal journey and ideas for happiness.

Elaine Hart, the former director of the Women's Opportunity Center, became bedridden for over a year with crippling arthritis. With plenty of time to think, she realized that her life spent in nurturing a family had helped them, but still left her with a feeling of wanting more. This strong-spirited woman overcame the debilitating illness and returned to college for her masters in counseling. Her subsequent work with the center touched the lives of many.

Luke (fictitious name), a former Philadelphia sales executive, continues each day to conquer the disease of alcoholism. "I learned to live at higher and higher levels of pain before I admitted my illness." Although he has lost his job in the process of treatment, the sales executive facade is beginning to crack. The real Luke has the first real chance in years to emerge ... and with that emergence will come true working and living.

## What Does It All Mean?

It means that sometimes we have to be thrown overboard before we can begin to make the choices that will allow us to truly be free to live.

But it also means that while there may be grief and mourning, sorrow and self-doubt, we'll never clamber back into the boat unless we reach for the gunwale and pull ourselves in.

It might be helpful to think of such an event in this frame of reference. A local minister once drew a dot within the middle of a large sheet of white paper. When he asked the congregation just what they saw, the answer came back loud and strong, "A black dot."

"Ah yes," he nodded sadly. "Did none of you see the white paper ... the big white sheet of paper that stretches well beyond this little dot?

"Your narrow focus on what is actually a very small, rather ugly speck on a much larger field of clean paper demonstrates just what happens when you channel all your energies and attention on a single unhappy or tragic event. The world and possibilities for happiness are truly much greater than you have recognized."

## Summary

1. A timely tragedy is one in which we are forced to deal with choices for our "work" and living.

2. The manner in which we allow ourselves to explore and expand our gifted-ness determines, to a great extent, just how fast we can move through and out of the timely tragedy.

# Chapter Nine
# Uppers, Downers and In-Betweeners

*Life is, without question, a fluid changing process
in which nothing is permanent or fixed.*

*– Carl Rogers*

Just last week we returned from ten days backpacking in the High Sierras, an annual family jaunt that had this flatland-bred lady scrambling over boulders, puffing up mountain passes, wading across turbulent snow-fed creeks, and counting shooting stars that whisk across a crowded night sky. When you're sleeping 11,000 feet above sea level, even new galaxies appear.

It occurred to me that this experience resembles, in many ways, the process of working and living. The trail carried me up peaks, down into valleys, across plateaus. Sometimes I stayed in one place longer than another, but eventually I had to move on. When it came time to thread our way up switchbacks, I knew that my water bottle better be filled and my walking stick in hand. Although each mountain pass was different, at least I was prepared.

That's the reason I felt a need for this chapter. In the process of making choices for balance and work/life, we all can expect to emotionally walk up, down, and across. BUT, if we know in advance that such movement is a natural part of the process, we might be better prepared for the road. Secondly, it might also be helpful to understand (and hopefully cultivate) some of the personal mind-sets which appear to promote quality working and living.

Let's first look at what emotions we might encounter in making choices for being faithful to our giftedness, our "work."

# Emotions

## Fear of Failure

It appears to me that there are two types of fear: pre-decision and post-decision. The first one keeps us nailed to the floor saying, "I can't." The second one keeps us running around in circles mumbling over and over again, "Oh #S%&%! What have I done?!" And both leave us depressed.

I spent about a year holding off writing a query letter to a publisher because I was afraid. Once I worked up enough courage to put my idea out for inspection, I was then faced with a signed contract and more fear. In fact, I probably wrote five drafts of the first chapter because I couldn't force myself to move into the book. Afraid again. Afraid that I couldn't cut the mustard, that I would be a failure. Oh, I didn't figure out what I was doing to myself for a while. I thought that it was just because I was too busy with my other work to find time to conduct interviews, to do the research and begin writing.

And then it hit. I was choosing to accept assignments rather than getting down to the real task at hand. I discovered that while I had successfully controlled (not canceled out) fear in the past, this was a bigger risk for me. I was holding on to some attitudes about myself which needed to be discarded: Everyone must like what I do or I am not acceptable.

Because I hadn't seen this attitude creep into my other work where I regularly face the public, deep inside I realized the tremendous personal importance of this book. Once I understood what I was doing to myself, I took steps to rearrange my thinking. I wrote affirmation cards that countered my old attitude. I turned down other work and cleared the decks for the book. And I took a deep breath and started—this time with real joy and renewed conviction.

Fear of failure might also keep us back from making choices for balance. Certainly fear is a primary emotion keeping Dr. O'Donnell and his fellow physicians from screaming "no more" to the unrealistic demands of a workload which takes every ounce of stamina.

Stephanie (fictitious name) is part of the senior management team in a powerful conglomerate. Taking her cue from her workaholic boss, she continues to carry home a briefcase filled to the brim with reports, rises before the sun is up to keep herself no less than two weeks behind schedule, and admits to doing the work of two or three people. Not only that, but she also sits on the board of nonprofit groups, attempts to make time for her lover and friends, and then crumples into exhaustion or nervous palpitations.

When asked why she doesn't call a halt somewhere, she says "I can't. Everybody has to work this way."

I would argue that she's working on a fixed view appraisal...seeing only one option. Only Stephanie can control the workload by either trying out various solutions or by really looking at her fear and what attitudes lie beneath the surface.

In many cases, we are not the only ones who can do the work. We might be the only ones who can do it in our particular manner, in our particular time frame, but there are others available for help. The thought of giving up some of our work to others might be threatening to our self-concept as powerful, fully capable people. The opposite is actually true. Giving up work which others might do actually empowers us to expand into other activities which are suited to our individual talents.

## Fear of Success

There's an equally common fear which is the exact opposite of what I experienced. The yang to the yin of failure is the fear of success. It is probably one of the most talked-about, read-about fears currently in the public eye.

As I see it, the core of this fear is a sense that with success comes lack of control, an imbalance, an upsetting of the apple cart when it comes to relationships, lifestyle, and maybe even personal values. The person grappling with this fear actually personifies "The Success" and gives it power to control his/her life.

Notice the verb "give." We only lose control when we choose to see ourselves as helplessly manipulated rather than being the manipulators.

# What to Do About It

*Worry is interest paid on a debt you might not owe.*

— *William Inge*

In reflecting about fear of failure and success, and considering my experience, I'm convinced once again that fear is made from a two-step recipe. The first ingredient is a crystal ball. The second is an attitude coated with feelings.

The crystal ball comes from our imagination where we project what might happen if we make a certain choice. Hours and hours of worry are spent anticipating something that might never happen. We look negatively and fearfully into the future.

We experience a feeling when we contemplate that imagined future. The deeper question which must be asked is this: What am I telling myself that is creating my response? Is this attitude, my perception of reality, something which is valid or is it time to change?

Fear can also be a good thing. Without fear we'd leap from buildings, walk across a burning tar pit, and jeopardize our well-being and maybe even that of others. As Benjamin Disraeli insisted, "Next to knowing when to seize an opportunity, the most important thing in life is to know when to forgo an adventure."

That's why it becomes terribly important to really challenge fear and test its true mettle. You might even luck out, as I did, and gain a new insight and a freeing attitude.

Like pits, fear comes in a variety of intensities ranging from mild worries to full-on phobias, the latter of which requires professional assistance. But for our purposes, may I share some general techniques which either I've found personally useful or which others have used. And we'll also turn to our case studies for more insight.

## Visualization

Mentally put yourself in the situation you fear, and this time imagine that you are really coping with your decision and maybe even enjoying it. (I visualized myself wrapping the book for a Christmas present; speaking from a podium and laughing with the audience; receiving letters from readers.)

## Jump Right In

Expose yourself, if possible, to that which you fear until you get over it. (I went to my office at 7 a.m., turned on the computer, and just plain began writing.)

## Worst Case

This is one of my favorite ones. I ask myself, "What would be the worst thing that could happen." Almost inevitably I realize that the "worst" case is that I die. Far worse is that I die without ever trying. There's a line in a prayer at my church that says "Forgive me for the things I have done and the things I have failed to do." The words, "failed to do" always strike the deepest regret within me.

## Reality Testing

Ask yourself if there is ample, real proof that whatever you fear might occur. (For example, I've never heard of an author getting hanged because some readers didn't like a book.) Make sure that you honestly assess the similarity between your situation and the test case. Ask an impartial third party to listen to your comparison for its validity.

## Get Away From It

Sometimes fear or worry can so clog the mental processes that nothing moves through it. Switch channels into something else like exercise, sleep, gardening, painting, reading, yoga, or whatever else might be your brain's Drano. "Sleep on it" has always been good advice.

## Comedy Capers

A sense of humor is really nothing more than a sense of perspective—clear, wide-angle perspective which allows us to rejoice in laughter at our own fallibility and that of others. Certainly Norman Cousins' now-famous illness must have initially carried tremendous fear with it—fear which he mitigated through humor. Even Lincoln is credited with this proclamation: "With the fearful strain that is on me night and day, if I did not laugh I should die." You might ask friends to help you find the silly, the absurd, the outrageous in your situation.

## Worry Things

This might be considered a way of combining a number of these techniques—everything from visualization to humor. Basically it implies that you put your fear or worry someplace else, that you move it out of your head and give it shape and form. I've seen people write the name of their fear on a rock and then throw it away. Others might draw their fear (probably getting a good belly laugh in the process) and then either burn the paper, or stick it away for another time. I've even seen worry dolls from Guatemala. These tiny figures, male and female, fit inside a small box and can be readily christened with the title of any fear or worry you wish.

By moving the fear into a place where you look at it, you regain control and perspective.

## Choices and Depression

Since this chapter is designed to prepare you for what you might experience, we do need to be aware that a significant work move cannot be made without evoking depression—here defined as loss, ambivalence, and of course, fear that things just won't work out. The longer you were with an organization, the closer your ties with fellow employees, the greater will be your sense of loss. Depending upon just what that new work choice is, you might also feel rootless, detached, and without direction.

Every time we leave something behind, we experience loss—and all loss must be mourned. If we take a clue from the hospice movement, words are necessary to dissipate sorrow. You must talk about the experience with people who can empathize without intrusion.

Depression might also come because our choices have not lived up to our expectations. True to form, the crystal ball and our imagination have done a number on us. It's time once again to try reality testing on our expectations and also to examine what might be that feeling-covered attitude. If I uncover an unrealistic expectation, my depression has no reason for being.

# For More Support With Fear, Depression and Choices

Whenever we chance to meet other backpackers on the trail, it is customary to exchange information about what lies ahead. There's much support and understanding in sharing mutual experiences. One is no longer alone. In fact, I'm glad to see other people looking as haggard as I do. Then I realize it's all part of the journey.

This brief collection of case studies is offered with the same spirit.

•••

*Sandy R., salesperson of industrial couplings.*

"The hardest decision I ever made was to leave teaching. I knew once I hopped out, I couldn't hop back. My confidence was very shaky and I was petrified. I think I just held my nose and jumped. And I became depressed after I left because the training program at my company didn't keep me busy enough. I was in limbo. Since I was following other salespeople around, I didn't have customers of my own and had no way of measuring my progress. In fact, I was laid off twice during the first year. The first time I was scared and the second time I was angry. But I stuck it out."

"I handle depression by giving in to it. I get it out of my system by wallowing in it: listening to the saddest music; crying all I want; and jogging. Then it vanishes."

"I've learned much in this process. Change is growth and anytime you move into the unknown you grow. The more self-knowledge you have, the more you have to give. Allowing yourself to grow in business and personal life is the only way you can say 'This is who I am.'"

•••

*Cheryl P., public-relations administrator and freelance writer.*

Once she determined to support herself with writing, Cheryl made adjustments in her lifestyle so as to lower the monthly income requirement. "But some days you think you're going to lose it all."

"But I keep going back to the fact that this is not a passing fancy but my decision. I'm doing it for myself. Sometimes, I laugh about fear and depression."

"I give myself mental pep talks, reminding myself that it's all worth the risk. It's something I've wanted for a long time."

"When I'm down, I tell myself that it's temporary, that it'll pass and it always does. And there's just not enough one can say about good friends, people who support, encourage and are just there for laughs, for counseling, even for objectivity."

"I figure that the worst which might happen is that I'll sell the house. Big deal. Besides [she laughs], I'd make a good waitress."

•••

*Bill E., former president of an outplacement firm.*

"After I was fired and opened my practice, I went to experiential workshops, meditation courses, positive affirmation courses—just a whole lot of things. It was lonely. That's why I selected an executive suite with other professionals and became involved in professional organizations. I needed the socialization."

"I was afraid of failure, financial insecurity. I didn't think I could take not getting a weekly paycheck. But building up a support network of other consultants helped considerably."

•••

*Charles D., counselor and video producer.*

"I hang in there, get through the anxiety and do it. It's been that kind of a process. I've been like a cat on a hot tin roof. Are people going to buy my services as a consultant? Am I going to make it as a psychologist?"

"Oh yes. Change is fearful. I always have fear with me but I've learned not to let it take control. When I recognize the signs, I talk to myself. 'Hi, fear. So you're going to be here awhile. Well, hang on while I do some self-affirmations.' I answer the fear back."

•••

*For Sunny F, now age 60, a multitude of fears arose around the time she made her crucial decision to leave the university and become a screenwriter.*

"In my 45th year, I was offered a chance to go to Bangladesh and write a documentary. I left, fully convinced that I would be dead within the year. You see, both parents died at 45. That was traumatic. I lived in a house in my teens where, when you came home, you never knew if your father was going to be alive or dead."

"I returned on my 45th birthday, certain that I had cancer. Instead, what I did have was a parasite from Bangladesh. When I realized that I wasn't going to die, I knew I had to decide what to do with the rest of my life."

"I decided, on my own, to come to California. By God I was scared. I was so damned scared that if someone had said 'boo,' I would've jumped 10 feet. I didn't know I could do this, but I knew I had to try."

"My brother kept telling me I was crazy. But I reminded him that our grandmother had walked out of Russia, clear across Europe, and came to the United States without even knowing the language. She survived. I can at least speak the same language. Why are you telling me I can't do it? What's the worst thing that could happen?

"I've never regretted coming here. It was like coming home."

## Exaltation

It's appropriate to follow Sunny's closing comment with the assurance that we may also expect to stand on mountain tops and shout "Eureka," keeping in mind that eventually we'll be moving down from the top and either into a plateau or valley.

I remember feeling tremendous elation, excitement, and the release of great pressure when I chose to move into my own practice.

And there have been other choices for living and balance which have merited equal exaltation: getting in my car and driving westward into an unknown future; marrying Bill; successfully going downhill skiing for the first time; receiving the acceptance call from the publisher.

One can live for days on such mountain tops. The important thing is that we keep alive the memory of such exaltation for those times when, as will inevitably happen, we are struggling with imbalance, a pit or even a pothole.

# Guilt

As you move through the process of working/living and unfolding your giftedness, some choices might be turned aside or diminished because we feel guilty about either making them or maybe even just thinking about them.

Like fear, the emotion of guilt covers an attitude which must be examined for its validity in your life. In making choices for the "work" of our lives, men and women alike must respond to an age-old premise: the man must be the provider; the woman must nurture and tend. And now, there's also a contradictory premise which challenges women to seek board rooms and men to change diapers.

Can you see how excessive guilt for not obeying either one of these cultural sex-role standards can lead to imbalance? Ever heard these?

Woman: "I graduated top in my field so I guess I'll go on. But I'd really rather stay home and have children."

Man: "I've got to keep this job to put my children through college. That's what fathers are for."

Woman: "I won't be a good mother if I don't prepare a hot, balanced meal every night."

Man: "My wife wants a vacation in Europe. I'd hate to disappoint her."

Woman: "My husband needs me to run the household. He'd never have clean clothes or matched socks if I didn't."

All of these sentiments are fine—if you are being faithful to yourself, if you are in balance, if you are happy. But if guilt is pushing your choice buttons, it's time to examine just how valid is that sentiment. There is nothing selfish in shifting responsibility, in seeking your own identity, in growing. I've learned that my husband does the wash much better than I, that salads are healthy, and that I don't want a gigantic business practice that takes me away from my family.

On the other hand, I've also observed where guilt has been so exorcised that true damage occurred to others, particularly children. The pursuit for self-growth is not something which takes place in a vacuum. And so it requires careful, honest evaluation to determine if our choices are made with integrity for all parts (and people) in our lives.

The feeling of guilt is not only attached to potential choices for change in sex roles, but it also can influence (if we choose) our balance in other areas of life. The password for letting guilt get the upper hand is "yes."

Case in point: I belong to quite a number of professional organizations, all of which understandably look to members for active participation. Up until last year, I kept nodding yes, sitting on a number of boards, chairing major projects, attending meetings, and trying to wear all the hats of independent consultant, wife, mother, and friend.

My head bobbed up and down like a yo-yo because I felt guilty if I did not actively participate. Underlying that guilt were other attitudes which said, "You will only be a good professional if you accept this work; you will not be liked if you turn down requests for help."

Wow! How's that for putting a real tilt on my working/living? I have now become very selective in my participation and have learned, in the process, that organizations and members do understand.

Knowing when to say "No, thank you" without guilt is a technique which we all could use. It becomes easier the more aware we are of what circles in our lives need reconnection or touching.

## Changing Identity – An Emotional Package

## FOR YOU

In the process of working and living, as we make choices for movement toward growth and life integration, we change – inside and outside. Values and self-perception, even standards of living might alter so that there's a new person staring back at us in the bathroom mirror.

All kinds of emotions present themselves when we look at this unfolding "us": wonder, celebration, delight, bewilderment. Of the many people I interviewed, only those who had yet to claim power and control over their out-of-balance lives viewed themselves with sadness and regret.

•••

*Sean F., the former still photographer-turned-outdoor-video-cameraman, shared his observations about his new identity.*

"I know I'm a different person ... gentler, more sensitive, less temperamental. I'm not primarily motivated by making a ton of money, unlike when I was younger. Now that the money is secondary to my enjoyment (living my adventures and experiencing nature), it quite frankly rolls in."

"In the past, for a few years, I earned as much as $10,000 per month. I bought houses, an airplane, fancy cars. Maybe it's okay for people to go through that. But those days are gone and I don't look back. Also at one time, it became an obsession to win awards. It fed my ego and at the time, I had a humongous ego. But that's over."

"I've gone through a real purification and I'm glad I've gone through it now rather than at 50. Now I can get on with my life. I don't require so much anymore. Little things make me happy."

## For Family and Friends

From Sean's story you can readily see how a change in identity, based upon a choice for his "work" influenced many areas of his life. Although he is currently not married, it takes little to imagine what impact his changed identity would have on a wife, family, and friends.

It is well to be aware that changing identity can arouse feelings of insecurity, jealousy, and loss in significant others. It can be the proving ground for marriages and friendships. In fact, dissension over choices for either our "work" or a "job" might really be rooted in deeper issues. Just read between the lines of the following statement:

"Other women seem to find fulfillment in running a beautiful home and doing charitable work. But not my wife. Instead of appreciating a successful husband who provides for her, she goes on and on about getting a job. My first wife wanted a job and so I gave in. Within one year she had a lover and left me. There's no way I'm going through that again. Someone needs to talk some sense into her."

Get the picture? Not only are there a variety of issues going on here, but it also appears that communication and active listening have been superficial at best.

Now that Richard G. has made the complete transition from probation officer to playwright, I asked him to tell me how his wife and seven children have managed his new identity and the attendant change in their lifestyle. During the conversation, it became apparent that he and his wife Carol have instilled a collective attitude in their family that influences everything from self-worth to money. It's an attitude which could only come from much open communication and sharing.

•••

*Richard G., playwright.*

"I know that even if I wasn't going to make money writing, I'd still be a writer because that's what I've discovered I am. I think our kids have that outlook. They know their worth and it's not a dollar bill. They are very self-sufficient and strong-minded about what they want to do with their lives. If we were totally about material things, my kids wouldn't have that."

"Carol knows how important this is. She had been after me for a couple of years to make the move. That's why I have a dedication in my book of poetry which says, 'A special thanks to my best friend and wife, Carol, who taught me that a true friend is willing to take a risk for you and will glory in your growth'."

"We don't have a budget like a lot of people do because, to us, a budget is very restrictive and says that you can't do what you want to do. Sometimes we get in trouble. Like right now our car has—no kidding—500,000 miles on it! But there are other things which are more important."

"Our kids know we don't have much money and they seem to appreciate what we do have. We're very close. Sometimes we might not be able to get the shoes we want because we've done something else, but we always get by. We're going to survive even if I didn't earn a penny from substitute teaching or writing. We would survive, life would to on. That's our attitude."

"I write in the den with the kids coming in and playing their records. Sometimes the youngest is on my lap. That's all right. I don't scrimp my energies when it's needed in the family."

"When I get afraid or depressed—which isn't very often—I talk to my wife. I'm not a closed person, but when I get depressed I do get quiet. And Carol will say, 'Okay, Richard. Let's talk.' She's perceptive to my moods and what-have-you."

●●●

A change in identity coming from a major work/life decision can also generate both positive and negative feelings in friends. In fact, as Richard penned in his poetry book, perhaps that is the mark of a real friend—someone who glories in your growth.

●●●

*When Carol Z., a single parent and lifelong educator, left her position as principal to become a management consultant, she discovered a mixed reaction.*

"By the age of 40, I reached burnout. Although I had managed to combine my beloved arts, dance and music into my work, I had reached a point of stagnation and overwork. A friend noted that I was giving 200 percent and it was killing me. He was right. It wasn't enough to know that I could go after and get a higher position with the county Department of Education.

"Once I left, the phone started ringing. Comments varied from 'that's great' to 'you're losing your mind.' A number of the principals and administrators expressed concern for my move. I think it was very threatening for them to think about making a change. And so many came up to me and said, 'You know, I wish I could do this."

"Interestingly, the PTA mothers seemed most traumatized. I had spent hours with these bright wonderful ladies but somehow they saw me as 'leaving them.' I think I was a role model and someone to talk to. I spent much time with a number of them after I made my decision. I think it forced them to focus on their own lives and ask things like: What am I doing? How much of me never gets listened to? What do I want? That latter question was probably the hardest."

## Personal Qualities

Throughout the interviews, I became aware that those individuals who were vitally aware of their life's journey, attempting to focus on the "work" of their lives, and consciously choosing paths for balance or temporary imbalance had at least three things in common: a willingness to risk, a high level of self-esteem and confidence, and faith in something or someone outside themselves.

## Willingness to Risk

When I was in high school, I memorized the poem If by Rudyard Kipling for some speech contest. While so much of it now escapes me, there still remains one line which continues to haunt my subconscious:

"If you could make one heap of all your winnings and risk it on a game of pitch and toss, and lose, and start again at your beginnings and never breathe a word about your loss...."

A powerfully strong image burned in my mind the first time I read that line, burned deeper the first time I presented it, and has been branded ever since. What continues to impress me even more than the idea of gambling all you have, is the concept of joyful risk. I can imagine no other reason for the absence of moaning, commiseration, and self-flagellation.

I saw this in so many of the people who kindly and courageously shared their personal journeys with me. The riskiest choices for quality living were made because of a deep-felt conviction that this was, in fact, the very thing that had to be done. So there was great joy in making the moves.

The willingness to risk contains one other component besides a joyful conviction: an acceptance of the unknown. Sunny F., a lady who has taken more risks than a daredevil, explained it best when she shared the tale of Brilliant Baby, an embryo awaiting birth.

Cuddled within his mother's womb, Brilliant Baby is busily taking notes about his remarkable development. "Oh, boy! Look at my feet. I can wiggle my toes. Aren't I something? Say now, watch me flex my arm muscle. I sure am a strong one. And hair, I've got fuzzy hair!"

In short order, the time had come for Brilliant Baby to be born. He feels pressure pushing him downward and he despairs. "Oh, no. I'm being forced out of the place. I'll be crushed in the darkness. I'm going to die!"

What a wonderful surprise is obviously in store for the tiny newborn. But without the birthing pressure, our fabled baby would have stayed exactly where he was. Often we do the same. Afraid of what we can't see or understand, we accept less than our full birthright.

There are two other points to consider under the willingness to risk. First, we each have our own perception of what is risky for us. That's a difference which must be accepted and appreciated in each other. What is a risk for me might be a piece of cake for you. Second, the bigger the risk, the bigger the growth.

• • •

*Mary G., now manicurist.*

"I think deciding not to go further in medical school was probably the biggest risk I ever took ... the family, future, status, wealth and everything that medicine promises. I'm no longer afraid to risk. If I could live through that, I figure I could probably live through anything. It's the whole idea of quitting once you've started. And I didn't have something else.

"I am who I am. I have no one else to be. I don't have any other script to work from. The only one I know well enough is me. So I can change things about myself, which I do continually. But being somebody else and living up to an image is something I already tried and it didn't work."

## Self-Esteem and Confidence

As a complementary attribute to the willingness to risk, growth seekers see themselves as people with possibility. Because they are joyfully eager to risk, their confidence level increases with new experiences. And, I think, many have created small wellsprings to use when their confidence lags.

They are not invincible. Rather, they are willing to accept the outcome of their choices without a loss to their sense of self. As Richard G. said, it didn't matter whether he was paid or not for his writing. All that mattered was that he knew it was right for him.

It would appear that individuals who have successfully discovered the "work" of their lives or are busily going about the discovery process, who maintain a rather steady balance, and who eagerly await the next day, have tapped deep into their well of being and found themselves not wanting. Self-esteem and confidence have allowed them to risk, be at odds with the crowd, and grow.

Confidence can also be a fickle quality, sometimes hiding when we need it most. I discovered that quite a number of people, including myself, keep a file of what Sunny F. calls TLC (tender loving care) notes. "You put in it all the warm letters, the thank yous, the congratulations. I think our insecurity in life pops up sometimes so that all we see are our lesser qualities. It's healthy to take out that file and remind yourself what you are doing right."

Lastly, confidence and a solid self-esteem permit us to accept new learning curves. Meeting manager Gary R. concludes, "I don't ever want to grow up. I figure that if I'm ever satisfied with where I'm at then I'm not growing anymore. I don't want to stop growing until I'm dead. I want new challenges. If you had asked me two years ago if I could/would do sales, I would've said 'Sorry, that's not my bag.' Now I'm finding out that it's fine."

# Faith

Do you recall the story of Marsha, the divorcee who put herself through a masters program and opened her own private school while also raising three sons? When I asked her how she managed that without giving into despair or depression, her answer came as no surprise, "I've always believed in the positive power of God. I know there's a larger force than I which will channel what I need."

The reason I was not surprised by her response is that the majority of people I spoke with all evidenced an awareness of both responsibility to a bigger world and the recognition of a Power beyond themselves. I call this awareness "faith."

I must admit, I hesitate to use the word "faith" because initially it implies an organized structure of beliefs with ritual and symbolic meaning. Rather, in responding to the giftedness of our life and in making choices for living, I see faith more in terms of a relationship. And there are many kinds of relationships with a Being, Force, or Power ranging from a deeply intimate and personal one to a barely nodding acquaintance. Some of us can name who or what we have a relationship with. Others cannot. What matters more is to respond with integrity to whatever relationship we claim.

Although the spiritual portion of our life is where we nurture that relationship, faith here also implies a more direct link and influence in our choices for working/living. If the Kingdom of God is within, as I firmly believe, then the process of becoming who we are meant to be is not only faithfulness but downright holiness. And in the process, we are not meant to see through each other but to see each other through.

You've already seen faith at work in some of the other case studies, but I felt a need to share these additional thoughts with you. Although there is a spectrum of faith relationships, it is nevertheless present for all these people.

•••

*Cheryl P.:*

"I don't have an organized religion, but I do have some inner faith that God is looking out for me. I pray sometimes but often not consciously. I believe in being good to people, in being honest. Yes, I have a faith."

•••

*Bill E.:*

"I've put together my own spiritually stimulating program because God is important. I even spent a couple of weekends in an ashram after getting fired. It strengthens your ability to understand anything. You get to God by looking at yourself and the more you look at yourself, the closer you get to God."

•••

*Ronda S.:*

"Faith in God is important for the celebrating of life. I find it's real important to me to go to church, to set aside that time. It's humbling to realize I am part of a bigger picture. It puts things in perspective. I'm a Methodist—it's a basic brick."

•••

*Richard G.:*

"We commute over the mountains to a church we've gone to for years. I get my faith from Carol. She's a preacher's daughter. Thanks to her, I've got a second dedication in my poetry book: 'A very special thanks for the love in the world and to the God who provides it.' And he does. We're always taken care of."

•••

*Sunny F.:*

"I believe that there is a power greater than me and we're all part of it. There's something stronger within us before you get to God. There's a greater us and that greater us is connected to God. I know we can all call upon ourselves to do things we never thought we could do."

"I think I believe in my heart that there are not questions without answers. If we have a question then the answer is somewhere. We might block the answer. Nor do I believe there is only one right answer. I think there are many paths we can take. None of them are right and none are wrong. They're just different."

•••

*Sandy R.:*

"I believe in an Omnipotent Power that makes sense out of all of this. You must listen to the inner voice."

•••

*Charles D.:*

"I have faith in all of us as part of the universe. My work allows me to do the give-backs to the world. All you have to do is to pass the baton to one person, to give one person encouragement. That's all we have to do to keep this universe going."

For me, I have a hard time separating faith from any part of my working/living process. And I'm not sure that within this book I could share the vital impact this relationship has had on accepting and forgiving who I am, on the opening and closing of doors in my life, on strength that comes from sources other than my own, on the presence of so many kinds of love that move like grace, and on faults and weaknesses that I can only claim as all mine. But this I do know: it is much easier to traverse mountains and streams when there's somebody bigger to take your pack or maybe even carry you across.

# Summary

1. Making choices for working/living and balance might be easier if we are prepared for some of the emotions which might help or hinder our sailing.

2. The fear of failure or the fear of success come from negatively viewing the future and responding with feeling-coated attitudes. Some attitudes might be worn out perceptions which do us more harm than good.

3. Some methods for handling fear are:

- Visualization

- Jump Right In

- Worst Case

- Reality Testing

- Get Away From It

- Comedy Capers

- Worry Things

4. Depression results from fear, from unmet expectations, or from loss. The more dramatic the work move, the more probable the loss—particularly if you have developed a significant history with the former place of employment and/or its people.

5. All loss must be mourned by dialogue.

6. You might, and hopefully will, experience exaltation with some "work" choices as well as choices in other areas of life. Keep that memory in a tinderbox for other times.

7. You might experience guilt over a potential change in cultural sex roles. Guilt also throws us out of balance when we can't say "no."

8. A change in work identity might prove the testing ground for marriage, family and friendships.

9. There are three common personal characteristics which appear in individuals who are successfully striving to achieve quality working and living:

- Willingness to Risk

- Self-Esteem and Confidence

- Faith

Food for thought along your voyage:

---

*Be patient to all that is unsolved and*
*love even the difficult question.*

*— Rainier Maria Rilke*

---

# Chapter Ten
# In Celebration Of the Journey

*It is good to have an end to journey towards;*
*but it is the journey that matters in the end.*

— *Ursula K. LeGuin*

Have you ever noticed that frequently the closing chapter of some books reads like a half-time pep talk? Go out and get that goal! Be a success! Win! Be tops!

The emphasis is on achieving an end result.

I guess I'm a little different. I think the victory (and living) is not based upon what you score but rather how you play. Think about it. If you could see your life stretching before you like a road, there would probably be monuments scattered here and there in commemoration of an achieved goal, a success. But between those glittering obelisks lie days of travel – days of your life.

Some of us go through life with our eyes glued on that monument, letting everything else around us slip by in a peripheral blur. We sit on the uppermost step of our monument, wipe our brow, and proclaim to the world "Yahoo! I've made it. Now I can be happy."

But what about all the time it took to get there? What happened to life in all those days and maybe even years when we were squinting at the distance and running toward some gleaming goal? What if life ended before we got there? Would we then never have achieved what it means to fully live?

Can you see why I feel so strongly that it is the daily sailing, the celebration of our journey, that is in fact the kernel of life?

I am not negating the very real presence of dreams toward which we aspire, goals toward which we aim. We must have a vision that keeps us growing, a vision of how we want our life to be and who we want to be in it. And, if we are to be truly free to live, we claim the power to choose to make it happen. The good news is that we don't have to wait until all the pieces come together before we say "Now, this is living."

Hopefully you picked up that feeling in many of the shared stories. People like Cheryl, Robert, Charles, Ronda and others expressed excitement over the fact that their lives were in process, not that they had arrived!

Let me share some other good news. Not only are we powerful people by having the ability to claim what goes into our life, by making choices for growth and balance, by moving through pits, by changing limiting attitudes, but we also have the magic of magnetism.

## The Magic Of Magnetism

This is my phrase for the simple tenet: you get back exactly what you put out. Or as Sunny F. phrases it, "Be careful of what you ask for—you might just get it."

While we have all heard that the power of mental imaging can do much with our physical bodies—walking unharmed on burning coals, creating illness, even death —it might come as a revelation to some that we also have the power to influence matters outside our skeletal framework. Specifically, it appears that when we begin to truly uncover the unique "work" which is ours alone to do, the Universe is there to support our effort.

I admit, it does sound all rather mysterious and magical, but I've personally and professionally seen too much to discount that reality. As soon as we begin to do that which energizes us and gives us meaning, a host of seemingly serendipitous people and things come to our aid.

Even when this book was but an untitled mental concept, I began to meet individuals whose stories I kept on file, not really knowing why I was doing it. Once I actively formulated the idea and plunged in, all manner of reference material and resource people suddenly (and I do mean suddenly) appeared. Whatever I needed, when I needed it, was somehow there. I did not plot, plan or belabor this effort.

Do you see the implication? Instead of worrying about reaching the goal of a finished book, it was merely enough to start the journey and to relish each new person and connection that appeared along the road.

I really feel it is so important to share this idea because frequently we have a tendency to say, "Well, those people are different from me so I guess I'll just have to stay as I am" or, "I can't do this." That's because we think we have to journey along. But we don't.

Don't take just my most recent experience as a sample. Let's look at some others.

•••

When Steve C. sold what he had to concentrate his efforts on his nautical museum and later reconstruct a period tall ship, The Californian, for use as a training vessel in the state's Youth Sail Training Program, the magic of magnetism went to work.

"During the building process, maybe even when we were in the jungles of Belize cutting timber, I received a call from the Coast Guard historian. It turned out that the model we were using for our design was The Lawrence, the first Coast Guard cutter to come to the West Coast. Not only that, but The Lawrence led directly to the formation of the Coast Guard Academy."

"That connection gave us needed publicity and we were named California's official tall ship and the lead vessel in the Olympic boat parade. When you're running a non-profit foundation, that exposure is vital. And thanks to such publicity, the Sacramento Redevelopment Agency has contracted with us to build another ship!"

For Martin W., the commercial artist whose loss of his business catalyzed renewed efforts in his beloved wildlife paintings, all it took was a resolution to change geographic locations for balance and his "work."

"I can't believe it. Everything has fallen into place. There are fewer jobs in Northern California, but thanks to my wife's former employer, she got a job with a wonderful woman doctor. She's excited about her work. Not only that, but one of the artists has offered me a position in his silk-screening business and we've got homes lined up to rent."

"This was all meant to be. I think I was being tested. Now I can paint not just whales but elk, raccoon and bear. Wildlife is almost like a faith to me. I really become energized by watching people look at my paintings and talk about the animals. Somehow I think they begin to see how we all—humans and animal—fit together. And I hope that the animals do some kind of spiritual talking to the people.

"I'm excited and scared. I'll still keep some commercial accounts in this area and they'll let me work on them even at a distance. That's another unexpected plus. I really do think this was all meant to be."

•••

*Charles D. expressed his experience in these terms:*

"It's been three years now and something has always worked. Making the commitment, with Providence stepping in, things did break. The free cable show which I started when I made the move now has me doing some video consulting. I've put some productions together and people are paying me. So television has evolved into some income which adds to my other work."

"Everything is coming together. I'm doing a documentary for the college and a documentary on divorce mediation. I'm going to be doing a special for the local medical school on Alzheimer's disease. That's the kind of thing I want to do."

"My strength is coming from my experience. As a counselor, I am what I am selling. I'm being me. I'm doing my part to make it happen and everything is unfolding. One thing is leading to another."

•••

In the unfolding of Sunny F's true work as a writer, she recounts numerous events of unplanned assistance.

A casual acquaintance placed the call which sent her scurrying to the university. "A friend tried to get a free truck since I didn't have enough money to move. He ended up renting a truck for $100, moving me to the college, and I never saw him again. And when I came to California, I found that I didn't even have enough to pay the van line. The owner of the hotel where my daughter and I were staying heard about my dilemma and handed me $1,000 in cash—just like that. No note."

"Ever since my experience at the university, I've believed that things are always there when I need them. The job with Disney, my Lockheed connection ... everything has happened at the right time. You get out of life what you put into it. In this terrible, heartless business of script writing, I have met some very wonderful people. I am where I belong."

•••

The magic of magnetism also works in reverse. An ancient legend tells the story of an evil king who sent his wise servant out to sow oats. But instead of oats, the servant planted wheat and so wheat grew.

The king was furious. He ordered the guards to seize the servant and bring him to the throne.

"Why did you plant wheat, you imbecile? I told you oats," the king thundered. "Well," replied the servant with his eyes downcast to hide their gleam. "I see you constantly sowing greed, anger, and evil yet expecting good to come to you. So, I naturally followed your wisdom and thought wheat would bring oats."

Now we don't have to be as overt as ye olde shag nasty king to wind up getting exactly what is our due. In fact ,negativism (my great bugaboo) can also hamper us from really getting the most out of our life. In fact, we can lose the moments.

I did such a thing on this most recent backpacking trip. My husband has a tendency to leave the well-worn trails and head cross country, proclaiming "I can't believe that someone hasn't done this before."

The first half of this particular trek was fit for mountain goats and ice-climbing acrobats. I grumbled and groused to myself from then on out. All I could think about was my aching back, the pain in my knees and feet, and the heat. By the end of the eleven-day trip, I was the last one off the mountain—a heap of misery and convinced that I was not cut out for such antics.

Within a few days after our return, when my heat rashes had cleared, the feet felt better, and my back could smile, I started thinking about the trip. Like a flash it occurred to me: Eileen, you did it to yourself!

Although I loved the days in camp, every time I shouldered that pack, I immediately concentrated on everything that was wrong. So I got exactly what I thought about—pain and misery.

What I had neglected to rejoice—yes, rejoice—about, was that I had successfully made it through each day, carrying more weight than I've ever carried, over rougher terrain than I've ever traveled. And the wonderful sights were certainly worth the effort.

Maybe like Martin, it was another lesson I just had to learn.

How often do we all go through our day's journey with only thoughts about everything that is going wrong? Why not pick out everything that is going right? Or at least congratulate ourselves on the effort? Not only do we reap a self-fulfilling prophesy with negativism, but we've lost a day of living.

## Toward a New Way of Thinking – Toward Now

Stand back with me for a minute, and let's look at where we've come. Work has been redefined as that which energizes us, uses our preferred skills, gives us meaning, and from which we draw a sense of self. It is the giftedness which we alone bring into the world, but it may or may not be the same as our job.

To truly live, we must become aware of how we are connected and balanced with all areas of our life, in addition to "work." A choice in one area of life carries impact in all and therefore we learn to sail. Whatever direction we head by our mental or verbal expectations, we will—in all probability—get there.

But if it is the journey which counts most toward living, then we must become people with a mind-set that shouts "Now!" We must become people of response rather than people of reflex. Response requires conscious behavior; reflex only requires autonomic reaction.

Whether we are, at this very second, shouting from a summit or struggling deep within a ravine, we hold all the resources to respond and truly live. For it is only by soaking in all the gamut of human feeling that we do, in fact, really live. There must indeed be winters in our life if we are ever to have springs.

When Arctic blasts move across the mountains, the higher elevations are scoured by gales, burnished by ice, and frozen beneath tons of snow. The miracles born each summer from that onslaught are fragile alpine meadows surrounded by granite cliffs. Here blossoms no bigger than a lentil nestle within the cracks of gray stone, accepting their moment in the sun.

This then is the final triumph of life—finding and living the moments. I'd like to think that the mountain flower's all-too-brief visitation with the sun is what keeps her protected and alive when the world becomes a swirl of cold.

Thus, not only must we celebrate our sailing and the journey itself, but we must also seek out and relish the moments. Corita Kent wrote truthfully when she insisted, "Love the moment and the energy of that moment will spread beyond all boundaries."

For the journeying is made up of moments which, unless we seize them, are gone.

At age 40, Beverly shared with me the wisdom gained from watching her 39-year-old friend die within a year from cancer.

"I took her with me on a business trip to New York because she had always loved that bustling city. Heretofore, my method of working was to fly in with just enough time to get to the meetings, do my thing, and then fly home again. Well, I watched her be in New York, taking great delight in sights, smells, sounds, and tastes. Seeing her reminded me of how much the city had to offer; how much I lost by only seeing my narrow world.

"Later on, when she was confined to a wheelchair, my husband and I took her to the beach for a picnic. We filled the basket with all her favorite junk food. What a delight! She seized that moment with us, the sand, the surf, the sea gulls, and the crazy food to truly live where she was right then and there.

"She died the next day.

"I now fly to wherever I'm going with an extra day to spare—just to relish where I am. I, a former workaholic, now take one day off in the middle of the work week to be with a friend, to have lunch, to make a moment that is tailored just for my soul. The truth is we must make allowance for the fact that moments are personal treasures."

What "moments" have you most recently experienced? Any today? Whether by chance or by plan, responding to those moments transforms the ordinary into the stellar.

Thank you, fellow travelers, for all the moments which have danced like sparklers in the sharing of this process for our mutual unfolding. I know we have already connected in our journey by mentally supporting each other's deep desire for a quality life and by empowering ourselves to make choices for attaining the "work" of our lives in concert with our total human existence.

Carry on.

# Recommended Reading

The challenge with a book list: it is out of date as soon as I write it. There are so many new books and guides to help us in the world of work. There are web sites, seminars, webinars, and coaches. Sigh. How do I help you?

Here's what I propose. I'll list now those books that I have found personally valuable. Then, if you will visit my web site: **www.eileenmcdargh.com**, I will keep an updated posting on new books I discover. We'll post the list next to this book (in my online store), and you can download it free.

Furthermore, if you'd like to receive updates, new information, and a published-when-the-mood-strikes newsletter, drop me a note at **Eileen@eileenmcdargh.com.** I'll write you back and we'll get you going!

Last thing. Would you write me and tell me what has been valuable for you? What helped you turn work frustration into work fascination? We'll help each other if we continue to share ideas and action steps. Write me at **mcdargh@aol.com** Use the tagline: Ideas and Insights from the book.

Many, many thanks!

# Personal Reading List:

Adams, Marilee, *Change Your Questions. Change your Life*, Berrett Koehler 2004

Baker, Marian, *Wake-Up Inspired – Fuel Healtheir Successand Love the Life You are Meant to Lead*, New Story Press, 2006.

Bronson, Po, *What Should I Do with My Life*, Random House, 2002

Freudenberger, H.J. with Richelson, G., *Burn-out: How to Beat the High Cost of Success*, Doubleday and Company, New York, 1980.

Fortgang, Laura Berman, *Now What?* Jeremy Tarcher, 2004

Jensen, Bill *What Really is Your Life's Work*, Harper Collins, 2005

Jensen, Bill *The Simplicity Survival Handbook*, Perseus Books, 2003

Johnson, Spencer, *The Precious Present*, Doubleday and Company, New York, 1984.

Kabat-Zinn, Jon, *Wherever You Go - There You Are*, Hyperion, 1993.

Kang, Lawler, *Passion at Work*, Prentice Hall, 2006.

Kaye, Beverly and Evans, Sharon Jordan, Love It. *Don't Leave It.* Berrett Koehler, 2004

Lindbergh, A., *A Gift From the Sea*, Vintage, New York, 1965.

Leider, Richard J. and Shapiro, David, *Repacking Your Bags*, Berrett-Koehler, 1995.

McGee-Cooper, Anne, *You Don't Have to Go Home From Work Exhausted*, Bantam, 1992.

Peppers, Cheryl and Briskin, Alan *Bringing Your Soul to Work*, Berrett Koehler, 2000

Percy, Ian *Going Deep in Life and Leadership*, Macmillan, 1997

Rechtschaffen, Stephan, *Time Shifting*, Doubleday, 1996.

Richards, Dick, *Artful Work*, Berrett-Koehler, 1995.

Rohrlich, Jay B., *Work and Love: The Crucial Balance*, Simon & Schuster, New York, 1980.

Salsbury, Glenna, *The Art of the Fresh Start*, Health Comm., 1996.

Sanborn, Mark, *The Fred Factor*, Waterbrook, 2004.

Schor, Juliet, *The Overworked American*, Basic Books, 1991

Scott, Cynthia, *Take This Job and Love It*, Simon & Schuster, 1988.

Sher, Barbara, *Wishcraft - How to Get What You Really Want*, Ballantine, 1985.

Sher, Barbara, *I Could Do Anything If I Only Knew What It Was*, Delecorte, 1995.

Sher, Barbara, *Refuse to Choose*, Rodale, 2006.

# Bibliography

Freudenberger, H.J., with Richelson, G. <u>Burn Out: How to Beat the High Cost of Success</u>. Doubleday and Company, New York, New York, 1980.

Kaiser, Robert Blair. "The Way of the Journal." *Psychology Today* (March 1981), (reprinted from Dialogue House): 6476.

Kaye, Dr. Beverly. <u>Up Is Not the Only Way: A Guide for Career Development Practitioners</u>. Prentice-Hall, New Jersey, 1982.

Pieper, J. <u>Leisure: The Basis of Culture</u>. Random House, New York, New York, 1963.

Rohrlich, Jay B. <u>Work and Love: The Crucial Balance</u>. Summit Books, Simon & Schuster, Inc., 1980.

Terkel, Studs. <u>Working</u>. Pantheon Books, New York, New York, 1972.

## The Guide for this Journey...

Since 1980, Eileen McDargh's mission has been to help organizations and individuals put talent, time and treasure together in service of GREAT work. She's playful yet purposeful about work, passionate yet prayerful about life.

Her keynote speeches and workshops are compelling conversations laced with stories and humor. Only call her if you want energy, truth, and action. Time is too precious for anything but authenticity.

Her other books include:

*The Resilient Spirit*
*Heart Talk for Staying Rightside Up in a World That's Upside Down* and

*Talk Aint' Cheap. It's Priceless.*

**www.eileenmcdargh.com**